Liberal Tyranny in Higher Education

Liberal Tyranny
in Higher Education

How You Can Fight Back

David L. Goetsch
and
Archie P. Jones

AMERICAN VISION PRESS
POWDER SPRINGS, GEORGIA

Liberal Tyranny in Higher Education
How You Can Fight Back

Copyright © 2009 by David L. Goetsch and Archie P. Jones

Published by:

> The American Vision, Inc.
> 3150 Florence Road
> Powder Springs, Georgia 30127-5385
> www.AmericanVision.org
> 1-800-628-9460

Printed in the United States of America.

Layout design by Luis Lovelace

Cover design by Adam Stiles

ISBN 13: 978-0-9840641-2-0 Paperback

DEDICATIONS:

FROM DAVID L. GOETSCH

To Savannah Marie Goetsch
You are the light in my life.

FROM ARCHIE P. JONES

To Mary,
Christian fighter against
Liberal Tyranny

CONTENTS

Introduction

> *"Congress shall make no law respecting an establishment of religion, or prohibiting the free exercise thereof; or abridging the freedom of speech, or of the press; or the right of the people peaceably to assemble, and to petition the Government for a redress of grievances."*
>
> —Constitution of the United States
> First Amendment

We begin this book with the First Amendment to the Constitution to emphasize the guarantees of freedom of speech and freedom of religion made in it. We wrote this book because these freedoms are being marginalized, suppressed, and even denied with increasing frequency in American universities dominated by liberal professors and administrators. The increasingly frequent persecution of Christians and conservatives on university campuses is why we chose to use the term "tyranny" in the title of this book. The unprecedented abuse Christians and conservatives are experiencing on university campuses is precisely that—tyranny.

A minor incident at George Washington University (GWU) represents just the tip of the iceberg when it comes to liberal tyranny on university campuses. Conservative students at GWU placed crosses on campus as part of a pro-life demonstration to mark the anniversary of the Supreme Court's decision in *Roe v. Wade* (1973). Soon thereafter they found that the crosses had been vandalized and defaced. If this type of childish misbehavior represented the worst of liberal abuse on university campuses, there would be no need for this book. Unfortunately, it does not. This incident, though minor, is not isolated. Rather, it was one small skirmish in a much larger campaign by the radical left to intimidate Christians and conservatives on university campuses. The GWU case involved nothing more than petty vandalism, but as we show throughout this book the left is willing to go well beyond being a nuisance in order to silence Christians and conservatives. In fact, intimidation and other more serious forms of persecution are becoming commonplace on university campuses in America. Further, they are being perpetrated by people who claim to be ardent supporters of free speech.

> James Bopp, general counsel for the James Madison Center for Free Speech, said that the act (vandalizing and defacing the crosses at GWU) was part of an "alarming number of acts of intolerance from the left. We've seen a lot of suppression on college campuses lately. This takes us down a dark road."[1]

The growing intolerance of the left is indeed leading us down a dark road, one that violates both the Constitutional guarantees of the First Amendment and the spirit of academic freedom.

Increasing intolerance on university campuses is why we wrote *Liberal Tyranny in Higher Education: How You Can Fight Back*. Our hope is that Christians and conservatives will read this book before sending their children away to college. In the environment that prevails on many campuses today, Christians and conservatives can enjoy freedom of speech and freedom of religion only to the extent that they are willing to fight for them. This book shows the types of persecution Christian and conservative students might be subjected to on the campuses of major universities. It also shows how you and they can fight back against that persecution.

HOW THIS BOOK IS STRUCTURED

Liberal Tyranny in Higher Education: How You Can Fight Back is presented in two parts. Part One consists of four chapters that chronicle how, in many cases, universities that are dominated by the left: 1) indoctrinate rather than educate, 2) deny higher education's Christian heritage, 3) practice the religion of secular humanism and its ethical corollary, moral relativism, and 4) make war on God, country, and conservatives. Part Two consists of three chapters that explain how you can fight back against liberal tyranny from three different perspectives: individual, parent, and student. The last chapter in the book contains a final word on liberal tyranny.

FIGHT BACK BUT FIGHT LIKE A CHRISTIAN

The inherent irony in fighting back against liberal tyranny on university campuses is that Christians must fight like Christians. Members of the radical left can view Christians as the enemy and behave accordingly, which they do. But as Christians, we must to bring a different perspective to the fight. Christians may view the liberals who persecute them as adversaries, but not as enemies. The evangelical aspect of the Christian's worldview requires that even while vigorously defending ourselves from persecution, we must reach out in a spirit of Christian love to those who persecute us.

As difficult as it can be on a human level to take this approach, Christians must always be mindful of the example Christ set on the cross when he entreated His Father to forgive those who had scourged, tormented, and crucified Him because they knew not what they had done. As Christians we should fight the good fight against liberal tyranny using every resource and strategy available to us. But everything we do to fight back against the persecution of the left should be done in a spirit of Christian love.

The easiest response for Christians who are being persecuted on university campuses is to circle the wagons and adopt a bunker mentality. In an article about the work of intellectual evangelist, Eric Metaxas, Marvin Olasky says he "criticizes those who 'hide in a separate Christian subculture' and 'lose the ability to communicate effectively with those who are outside.'"[2] According to Metaxas, who is known for reaching out to the cultural elite,

> We become less and less able to speak to those who are different from us. That, of course, is the enemy of evangelism. We grow more and more fearful and suspicious of those outside the camp, until we slowly begin to think

of them as a hostile other whom we must destroy, rather than broken and exiled parts of our own selves, whom we are commanded by God to heal and restore.[3]

In Part Two of this book, we provide numerous strategies for fighting back against liberal tyranny. As you study these strategies and decide which of them you will apply, remember the words of Eric Metaxas. Christians will gain nothing by adopting the same low tactics used on them by the radical left. In fact, they will lose much more than they will gain and what they will lose is more important than any short-term gains they might enjoy. As a Christian concerned about liberal tyranny on university campuses, fight back, but fight like a Christian.

NOTE TO READERS

Throughout the remainder of this book there are occasional first-person comments and examples used. When this is the case, they should be attributed to David Goetsch.

NOTES

1   Mark Chenoweth and Michael Drost, "Conservative student groups decry 'intolerance' on the left," *Washington Times*, February 9, 2009.

2.   Marvin Olasky, "Mission to Metropolis," *WORLD Magazine*, February 14, 2009 (Vol. 24, No. 3), 63.

3.   Olasky, "Mission to Metropolis," 63.

Part One:

LIBERAL TYRANNY IN HIGHER EDUCATION

One

Liberal Tyranny in Higher Education:
An Overview

"The tyranny of the Zeitgeist in the matter of evolution is over-whelming to a degree of which outsiders have no idea."
—Thomas Dwight, Harvard University

O ne of the more liberal justices to serve on the United States Supreme Court was William O. Douglas. But Justice Douglas was prescient when he said: "Restriction on free thought and free speech is the most dangerous of all subversions. It is the one un-American act that could easily defeat us."[1] One cannot reflect on this quote without a measure of trepidation. In fact, the simple but powerful truth it conveys causes us to fear for the future of higher education in America and, by extension, for America itself. Make no mistake about it, the two futures are inextricably linked. We fear for our country's leading universities because they are perpetrating tyranny by suppressing free thought and free speech. The targets of this kind of abuse are Christians and conservatives. By suppressing the free thought and free speech of this substantial segment of America's diverse population, these universities are undermining the very purpose of higher education. David Horowitz summarizes this purpose as follows:

> The central purposes of a University are the pursuit of truth, the discovery of new knowledge through scholarship and research, the study and reasoned criticism of intellectual and cultural traditions, the teaching and general development of students to help them become creative individuals and productive citizens of a plu-

ralistic democracy, and the transmission of knowledge and learning to a society at large. Free inquiry and free speech within the academic community are indispensable to the achievement of these goals. The freedom to teach and to learn depend upon the creation of appropriate conditions and opportunities on the campus as a whole as well as in the classrooms and lecture halls. These purposes reflect the values—pluralism, diversity, opportunity, critical intelligence, openness and fairness—that are the cornerstones of American society.[2]

To undermine the purpose of higher education by suppressing Christian and conservative worldviews is nothing short of what Professor Dwight of Harvard University called it: tyranny. It is tyranny to God, our country, the university itself, and the students and professors whose views are censored and suppressed.

Do All Institutions of Higher Education Suppress Christian and Conservative Worldviews?

The title of this book is *Liberal Tyranny in Higher Education,* which begs an obvious question: Do all institutions of higher education in America practice the types of abuse and suppression described in these pages? The answer to this question is "no." There are still colleges and universities that do an excellent job of fulfilling both the spirit and letter of higher education's mission; institutions that still teach students *how* to think rather than *what* to think. I have worked at such an institution for almost 35 years as a professor, department chair, division director, dean, provost, and vice-president. There are others across the country that maintain the integrity of their missions in spite of the examples set by flagship institutions in this era of liberal domination of colleges and universities.

If you are reading this book and work at a college or university that is still committed to the fundamental mission of higher education, do not be offended—I am not talking about your institution. This book was written in response to what is happening at the majority of our country's flagship universities, those that set the tone and lead the way in higher education. These universities tend to be the larger institutions of higher education in their respective states, although many smaller institutions have followed their lead. These well-known and highly respected universities are now dominated by liberal faculties that are silencing Christian and conservative students and professors as they seek to consolidate power and advance their leftist agendas.

SUPPRESSING CHRISTIAN AND CONSERVATIVE WORLDVIEWS

In an op-ed piece for *The Washington Times,* Jason Mattera had this to say about how Christians are treated on college campuses: "Did you hear the one about a college student threatened with expulsion for handing out copies of *The Communist Manifesto*? Ha! Of course you didn't. When was the last time a campus official violated his fealty to leftist orthodoxy?"[3]

Mattera's article is about the case of Ryan Dozier, a student at Yuba College in California who was disciplined for handing out Christian pamphlets. The college's president gave Dozier a choice: stop handing out Christian literature or face disciplinary measures. Like many institutions of higher education, Yuba College attempts to corral free speech by forcing it into designated *free speech zones* and requiring permits of those who wish to exercise their First Amendment rights in these zones. At Yuba College, religious or ideological speech is restricted to the free speech zone for just one hour on Tuesdays and Thursdays.

As a college administrator, although I do not agree, I understand fully the desire of educational institutions to designate so-called free speech zones. It is simply a practical response to a growing problem: the disruption of teaching, learning, and campus life. University campuses are favored sites for those who wish to protest against any and all issues as well as for advocates of every socio-cultural cause known to man. Regardless of the issue, protestors and advocates have two things in common: 1) *they are loud,* and 2) *they are disruptive.* This forces university administrators to seek a balance between encouraging free speech and protecting teaching, learning, and campus life from disruption.

The other side of this issue is that although the exercise of free speech can be loud, disruptive, and even obnoxious, accommodating it is called democracy. Taking steps to protect teaching, learning, and campus life from disruption is an appropriate undertaking for a university administrator. However, using free speech zones to suppress free speech is not. After all, the entire university campus should be a free speech zone. Where Yuba College erred and where other institutions are erring is in using the concept of free speech zones to limit free speech. The trend is to locate free speech zones in isolated areas of the campus as far away from student traffic as possible and to limit certain kinds of speech to tightly restricted times and days. Another error universities are making is treating non-disruptive activities in the same way they treat disruptive activities.

There is nothing disruptive about handing out Christian literature on a university campus. It does not involve loud, haranguing speeches, large, boisterous crowds, or any of the other disruptive activities university administrators claim to be protecting students from by establishing free speech zones. In spite of this, Dozier was threatened with expulsion.[4]

This is not an isolated case. As you will see throughout this book, the Dozier case is representative of what is happening at colleges and universities nationwide. In writing about this issue, Dr. D. James Kennedy said:

> Like the Nazi threat of little more than a half-century ago, the current penchant for hating individuals because of their religious beliefs concerns not just the immediate targets of scornful persecution but eventually the entire social structure if allowed to go unchecked. Evangelicals and fundamentalists arouse passions and prejudices more than any other social group or minority, based entirely on what they choose

to believe under the aegis of the same Constitution that established liberty for every American citizen.[5]

GROWTH OF THE ANTI-CHRISTIAN MOVEMENT IN AMERICAN UNIVERSITIES

The anti-Christian movement on university campuses grew out of the debate between creationism and Darwinism. It began in Europe in the 1800s and eventually spread to America, but was slow to gain a foothold. Creationism did not begin to be eclipsed by Darwinism in America until the years following World War II. It was during the late 1950s that Darwinism began to appear prominently in textbooks. During the 1970s, Darwinists began to attack the teaching of creationism as *indoctrination,* the very claim that Christians now lodge against them.[6]

Eventually, through retirements and normal attrition, Darwinists gained the upper hand on university campuses and quickly moved to consolidate their power and perpetuate their control. Darwinists have been so successful in gaining control of university faculties that proponents of creationism or intelligent design must now keep their views underground in order to earn tenure or even retain their positions. In the irony of ironies, a prominent Russian scientist claimed in 1990 that there was more academic freedom in the Soviet Union than in American universities:

> In a time of *perestroika,* the academic freedom in Moscow and Leningrad looks better than in California. We have a real opportunity to carry out biological research in the creationist field, to organize public debates, scientific meetings, publications, lectures, and even to teach creationism as a *scientific subject.*[7]

Of course the principal argument made by Darwinists against creationism and intelligent design is that they are not scientific subjects. This is a patently false argument since Darwinism is based on the religious presuppositions of secular humanism and deals with the origin of life, a phenomenon which due to its very nature cannot be observed by scientists.

As liberal professors became more and more the norm in higher education during the 1980s, the deification of Darwin spread from university science departments to all departments. When left-leaning professors were comfortable that their domination of faculties was sufficient to allow it, they began to actively suppress Christian and conservative thought, inquiry, and speech, which is where things stand now.

ANTI-CHRISTIAN AND ANTI-CONSERVATIVE
ABUSES IN HIGHER EDUCATION

To understand just how far universities that once taught creationism have strayed from their roots, one need only consider the types of anti-Christian abuses that are now common in higher education. The Young America's Foundation compiles a list of the most egregious abuses every year. The latest list of abuses includes the following:

- *Anti-Military Bias at Columbia University.* Columbia University asked students to vote on a proposal to return Navy Reserve Officers' Training Corps (ROTC) to campus after an absence of 40 years. According to university officials, the referendum was defeated by 39 votes. However, a closer look at the process revealed a number of irregularities and questionable practices. For example, the university closed down online voting at different times for different students and discarded 1,900 votes out of a total of 4,905 cast. The university even admitted that one student had voted 276 times.

- *No Praying Allowed at the College of Alameda, California.* When Kandy Kyriacou, a student at the College of Alameda, visited her professor to deliver a Christmas gift, she found the professor ill. Concerned, Kyriacou offered to pray and the professor agreed. However, when another professor walked in to find the student praying for her sick professor, the fireworks started. The offended professor complained and Kyriacou soon received an "intent-to-suspend" letter for engaging in "disruptive or insulting behavior." This is what Christian prayer has become in many American colleges and universities: "insulting behavior."

- *Christmas Decorations Not Allowed at Florida Gulf Coast University.* Claiming he did not know how to celebrate Christmas in ways that honor and respect all traditions, the president of Florida Gulf Coast University eliminated all traditional Christmas decorations including holiday decor and greeting cards. Traditional Christmas celebrations were replaced with an ugly sweater contest. Fortunately, when his ridiculous actions were made public, the university's president had a change of heart.

- *Transgendered Guest Speaker at West Point.* West Point, with its tradition of duty, honor, and country, is the last university one would expect to allow its students to be subjected to leftist activism. Unfortunately, even the Corps of Cadets is not immune. A professor of Behavioral Sciences and Leadership on the military academy faculty invited West Point alum and transgendered male, "Allyson" Robinson, to class as a guest speaker. The former Mr. Robinson decried the conservatism of West Point's student body—the Corps of Cadets.

- *Pro-Life Speakers Not Welcome at a Catholic University.* The official position of the Pope is decidedly pro-life, yet pro-life speakers are not welcome on the campus of the University of St. Thomas, a Catholic institution. The university had already presented such leftist icons as Al Franken, the liberal comedian turned politician, and "Debra" Davis, a transgendered activist who claims that God is a black lesbian, to their students as guest speakers. But when it came to inviting pro-life speaker, Star Parker, the university balked, ignoring the concepts of "diversity" and "pursuit of truth" contained in its mission statement. When the issue threatened to become a public-relations nightmare, university administrators eventually reversed themselves and issued the invitation, but not before making it clear which side of the abortion issue they support.[8]

DO LEFTIST FACULTIES THINK THEY ARE IMMUNE TO CRITICISM?

One of the reasons I fear for the future of higher education in this country is that universities have become so out of touch with society that they seem incapable of understanding that a backlash is in the making. Liberal faculties in American universities remind us of the crew of the Titanic, sailing confidently into dangerous waters convinced their ship was unsinkable. In a society that is still approximately 70 percent Christian, universities cannot expect to condone anti-Christian abuses without generating pushback from the public, and this is precisely what is beginning to happen.

According to A. Lee Fritschler, Bruce L.R. Smith, and Jeremy D. Mayer, authors of *Closed Minds: Politics and Ideology in American Universities*,

> there should be no surprise that critics are taking a closer look at higher education than before. Some claim they are overpriced and wasteful; others decry that graduates are not adequately prepared. And echoes of older critics remain, as some allege that universities still discriminate in admissions and lower income students cannot gain entry. If they do, they graduate with nearly unmanageable debt. Although these criticisms are serious, probably the most frequent attack on higher education today is the accusation that universities, and certainly the elite institutions, are controlled by liberals who proselytize in the classroom, lower the grades of conservative students and discourage or even forbid debate. If in fact, liberal groups of faculty have gained control of universities and its classrooms the damage done to the academy would be severe. The critics' com-

plaints go to the heart of the mission of the university and, if true, need to be corrected directly and quickly.[9]

The research of Fritschler, Smith, and Mayer revealed that more than 70 percent of university professors self-identify as being either "liberal" or "very liberal." Even with this, the researchers attempt to downplay the effects of left-leaning faculties. Rather, they are more concerned with how universities respond to the criticism they receive when leftist abuses become public. "We concluded that, ironically, the universities have become more cautious in hiring faculty from the far left or right. Better to stick to the middle and to the scholar more interested in research than to stir what could become an unpleasant public debate."[10] One might reasonably ask, unpleasant for whom? I am sure that Christians and conservatives would welcome such a debate. In fact, part of the criticism of left-leaning universities is that worthy debates such as this have been silenced, suppressed, or otherwise precluded. Perhaps George Orwell said it best: "If liberty means anything at all, it means the right to tell people what they don't want to hear."[11]

HOW LIBERAL FACULTIES SUPPRESS CHRISTIAN THOUGHT, SPEECH, AND INQUIRY

Jerry Bergman presents eight tactics liberal faculties use to suppress Christian thought, speech, and inquiry in his book, *Slaughter of the Dissidents*.[12] These tactics can be summarized as follows:

- *Derogatory and belittling comments.* Derogatory and belittling comments made by professors, especially those made during class and in the presence of other students, can have a powerful effect on those at whom they are directed. Labeling a Christian or conservative student's views "ridiculous," "stupid," "bigoted," or "narrow-minded" hardly encourages free thought, free speech, or free inquiry. Yet inappropriate comments such as these have become commonplace in university classrooms. Christian and conservative students in America's flagship universities soon learn that they speak their minds at their own risk.

- *Denial of admission to graduate school.* Complaints in the literature as well as court cases suggest that Christians and conservatives, especially those who have been vocal in their rejection of Darwinian evolution or even moderately supportive of intelligent design, are being denied admission to graduate school. The denials are issued in spite of the fact that the Christian and conservative students in question have high scores on the Graduate Record Examination (GRE). This is an especially effective tactic because it has the salutary effect—from the liberal point of view—of limiting future applicants for professorships to Darwinists. No graduate degree, no professorship.

- *Refusal to award degrees.* This is a corollary to the previous tactic used just in case a Christian or conservative student somehow slips through the admission process. The goal is the same: keep the "club" liberal in its orientation by denying access to those who are not liberal. Again, based on the literature and court cases, Christian and conservative students who have met all academic requirements are being denied degrees on the basis of their creationist views or support of intelligent design.

- *Denial of promotions.* In spite of the efforts of liberal professors to deny Christian and conservative students the degrees they have earned or admission to graduate school, some still slip through. Consequently, there must be another tactic for limiting the impact of professors whose leanings are not sufficiently to the left. One such tactic is to deny them promotions. When liberal professors control university faculties—which is now the norm—they can also control who is promoted and who is not, irrespective of scholarly merit.

- *Censorship of literature critical of Darwinism.* Denying students access to materials on creationism and intelligent design is a favorite tactic of the left. One of the ways they accomplish this is by censoring what materials are placed in their university's library collections. When liberal professors control the faculty, they are able to use their clout to ensure that books which are not, in their view, worthy of study do not make it into the library collection. By claiming that creationism and intelligent design are not science—despite the fact that modern science was founded on the basis of Christianity and that the founders of every branch of modern science were Christians—they are able to keep books that question Darwinism out of library collections where students might read them and, as a result, ask troubling questions.

- *Denial of tenure and terminations.* In a major university, denial of tenure is the academic equivalent of the death sentence. The number of professors who are denied tenure as a result of advocating creationism or intelligent design is growing. The key decision makers in the award or denial of tenure are the departmental colleagues of the professor in question. If left-leaning professors who are pro-Darwin control the department, they are able to blackball professors who are proponents of creationism and intelligent design, in spite of their meritorious records. Once tenure has been permanently denied, the next step is termination.

- *Demotions.* One of the problems faced by left-leaning departments in universities is what to do about their creationist and pro-intelligent design colleagues who are already tenured. Once tenured, it is difficult to terminate a professor, regardless of his political or religious views. However, if liberal professors control the department in question, they still have an effective tactic available to them: demotion. Tenured professors in universities continually compete to teach the more prestigious graduate courses in their fields.

Teaching freshman and sophomore courses is often relegated to graduate teaching assistants. However, when a left-leaning department wishes to punish a faculty member for refusing to toe the Darwinist line, demoting him to teaching introductory-level courses is an effective and increasingly prevalent tactic.

- *Threats and intimidation.* At times, the feuds within departments of major universities get ugly. Christian and conservative students, professors, and guest lecturers report receiving threats and being the victims of all forms of intimidation, ranging from petty provocations to more serious actions. For example, it is not uncommon for conservative speakers on university campuses to be shouted down and even pelted with pies, excrement, and bottles. Intelligent-design advocates have received death threats. In his book, *Be Intolerant Because Some Things Are Just Stupid,* Ryan Dobson reports having his tires slashed on ten different occasions for voicing his Christian views.[13]

We will go into the left's war on Christians and conservatives in more detail in Chapter 4. At this point, suffice it to say that there is a war underway on university campuses and the left is winning.

WHAT SHOULD CHRISTIANS
AND CONSERVATIVES BE ABLE TO EXPECT?

Do Christians and conservatives have to sell their souls to get a good education in America? Do they have to check their values at the door of a university campus? Do Christians have to choose between winning in the classroom and losing their faith? We are asked these types of questions all the time, and our answer is always the same: a resounding *NO.* The freedoms granted to all Americans in the Constitution, including freedom of speech and freedom of religion, are on the side of Christians, even on university campuses. However, I am always quick to add that Christians who wish to exercise these freedoms in today's university environment should be prepared to fight the good fight. Part

Two of this book contains our recommendations on how to carry the fight for your rights into the lion's den—and win.

Ideally, every Christian's vision would be: "An America that recognizes the sovereignty of God over all of life and where Christians exercise servanthood leadership in every area of society."[14] This is the vision of the publisher of this book, and it is one every Christian should adopt. This vision will not be realized if Christians and conservatives simply give up and cede control of universities to the radical left. If Christians are going to fulfill their God-given dominion mandate, they must first fight to regain it. America's institutions of higher education represent one of the key battlegrounds in this struggle.

On the other hand, an America that once again recognizes the sovereignty of God is a vision that could take a good while to bear fruit. While work is underway to achieve this vision, there are thousands of Christian and conservative students who, in the interim, must decide what to do about college. This being the case, Christian and conservative students and their parents can be forgiven for asking: "What about right now? What should we be able to realistically expect from universities in the short term?"

Short-Term Expectations of Universities

Christian and conservative students should be able to attend any institution of higher education in America with full assurance that their values and rights will be respected. More specifically, they should be able to expect universities to live up to the bedrock values of higher education, values that include: the pursuit of truth, free inquiry, free speech, free thought, pluralism, respect for diversity, openness, and fairness. They should be able to expect an environment in which the following assumptions are true:

- Faculty members are hired, promoted, and granted tenure on the basis of competence and merit. Further, political and religious views are not detrimental factors in the hiring, promotion, or tenure approval processes.

- Students are graded solely on merit, not on the basis of their religious or political views.

- Students are granted admission to graduate studies on the basis of merit, not their religious or political views.

- Students are exposed to a wide range of worldviews, encouraged to think critically about them, and expected to arrive at their own conclusions. Dissenting opinions are both welcomed and encouraged.

- The teaching and learning environment is conducive to the civil exchange of ideas so that students and professors may disagree without being disagreeable. Academic freedom and intellectual pluralism are practiced in ways that ensure the integrity of the teaching and learning environment.

- Differing points of view may be expressed with full assurance that they will be given a forum and accorded the respect they deserve.

Universities that cannot assure students that the assumptions above are true in actual practice are not living up to their obligations as institutions of higher education. All students should be able to rely unequivocally on the reality of these assumptions, and now more than ever before.

Today's college graduates enter a world that is vastly different from the one their predecessors encountered after college. Summit Ministries sums up this situation as follows:

> Today's students enter a world of runaway biotechnology, postmodern social constructions of gender, virtual online identities, family redefinition, distorted understandings of beauty, and multiple sexual orientations, each of which fundamentally challenge our concept of humanness. Further, our culture has largely embraced Darwin, trivialized Scripture, and relativized truth,

and therefore left few stable resources to negotiate this corporate identity crisis.[15]

No wonder today's college-age generation is confused. It should be. Universities have no business adding to the confusion by undermining the one worldview that equips people to navigate the moral fog generated by America's cultural identity crisis. Dealing with these confusing cultural issues requires developing an understanding of what it means to be human, which in turn is part of what God reveals to us in Scripture. Attacking, reviling, and suppressing the views of those who seek answers to the questions surrounding these issues in Holy Scripture is behavior unworthy of an institution of higher education.

NOTES

1. William O. Douglas, as quoted in Louis E. Boone, *Quotable Business,* Second Edition (New York: Random House, 1999).

2. "Academic Bill of Rights." Retrieved from www.taup.org/taupweb2006/hr177/aborhorowitz.pdf on May 8, 2009.

3. Jason Mattera, "Abuse in academia?," *The Washington Times*, December 16, 2008.

4. Mattera, "Abuse in academia?"

5. Dr. D. James Kennedy, as quoted in Jerry Bergman, *Slaughter of the Dissidents* (Southworth, Washington: Leafcutter Press, 2008), xii.

6. Francis J. Beckwith, "A Liberty Not Fully Evolved? The Case of Rodney LeVake and the Rights of Public School Teachers to Criticize Darwinism," *San Diego Law Review,* pp. 1311-1326. Retrieved from http://www.discovery.org/articleFiles/PDFs/Beckwith_on_ID_in_SDLR.pdf on April 24, 2008.

7. Dmitri Kuznetsov, "An Open Letter to Bill Honig," *Acts & Facts* (Vol. 19, No.3, 1990), 1-3.

8. Young America's Foundation, "PC Campus: Academia's Top 10 Abuses of 2008." Retrieved from http://yaf.org/blog/?p=163 on January 19, 2009.

9. Young America's Foundation, "PC Campus: Academia's Top 10 Abuses of 2008."

10. A. Lee Fritschler, Bruce L. R. Smith, and Jeremy D. Mayer, *Closed Minds? Politics and Ideology in American Universities* as presented in "Civic Education, Not Right or Left Education," Jack Miller Center. Retrieved from http://www.jackmillercenter.org on January 3, 2009.

11. Fritschler, Smith, and Mayer, *Closed Minds?*

12. As quoted in Jerry Bergman, *Slaughter of the Dissidents* (Southworth, Washington: Leaf-cutter Press, 2008), xi.

13. Bergman, *Slaughter of the Dissidents,* 3–5.

14. Ryan Dobson, *Be Intolerant Because Some Things Are Just Stupid* (Carol Stream, IL: Tyndale House, 2007), 59.

15. From the vision statement of American Vision. Retrieved from www.AmericanVision.org on January 29, 2009.

16. John Stonestreet, "Why Students Don't Get It." Retrieved from http://www.summit.org/resources/essays/2009/01/why_students_dont_get_it.php on January 19, 2009.

Two

Denying Higher Education's Christian Heritage

"To destroy a people, you must first sever their roots."
—Alexander Solzhenitsyn

The historical record is clear—America was founded on Christian principles. To question this fact is to be grossly ill informed, in a state of willful denial, or have an anti-Christian agenda. Gary DeMar confronts the issue of denying America's Christian heritage in his book, *America's Christian History: The Untold Story*.

> The historical record is available for all to see. America's Christian history is a fact. No amount of redefinition or tampering with the historical record ought to be used to prove otherwise just so differing opinions are not offended. It was America's moral choice that made this nation the envy of the world and a haven for the oppressed.[1]

An interesting aspect of DeMar's statement is the irony implicit in the last sentence when one considers contemporary circumstances. America's Christian heritage made it "a haven for the oppressed." Yet in universities today it is often Christians and conservatives who feel oppressed. Just as America was founded on Christian principles, so were America's universities; although this fact is unknown to many who are indoctrinated in left-leaning schools in which *freedom-FROM-religion* is taught as gospel. America's first colleges grew quite naturally in a

Christian society which honored intellectual achievement as an important means of glorifying God, required much of its students, demanded a learned clergy, and was—as the books it published show—interested in virtually every area of life.

To get a feel for how far many of our flagship universities have strayed from their roots, contrast daily life at Harvard in its early days with the climate that prevails there today. Writing about Harvard's early days in his book, *The Search for God at Harvard*, Ari Goldman says:

> Religion was so much a part of everyday learning in the early days of Harvard that for nearly two centuries no one thought of setting up a separate Divinity School. In the college, students gathered daily for prayer and readings from the Scripture. Hebrew as well as Greek were required subjects, because an educated person was expected to be able to read the Bible in the original tongues.[2]

That today's college students are ignorant of the Christian heritage of higher education is not surprising. American students are increasingly out of touch with all aspects of our nation's history, a sad situation unto itself but not the most disturbing part of the problem. After all, ignorance is curable. The more significant aspect of the problem is that even when they know their history, many students have been conditioned to deny it or be ashamed of it. Rather than being taught to seek the truth, they have been misled by a left-leaning education system that has an anti-Christian, anti-conservative agenda.

In many universities today, to advocate a fair hearing for the truth of the historical record is to bring the wrath of the system crashing down on you. This overt anti-Christian crusade is a fairly recent development. Universities in this country have a long history of being more liberal than the American public at large—there is nothing new in this. However, their propensity for condoning and even encouraging the suppression of Christian and conservative points of view is a relatively new development that has emerged gradually since the end of World War II.

What is happening on the campuses of many major universities today is downright Orwellian. The slogan of Big Brother in Orwell's classic book, *1984,* was: "Who controls the past controls the future. Who controls the present controls the past." Through the persistent and effective application of revisionist history, liberal faculties are controlling the present so they can control the future. Patrick Buchanan speaks to this Orwellian strategy in his book, *The Death of the West:*

> Many of the institutions that now have custody of America's past operate on the principles of Big Brother's Ministry of Truth: drop down the "memory hole" the patriotic stories of America's greatness and glory, and produce new "warts-and-all" histories that play up her crimes and sins, revealing (or, more accurately, portraying) what we have loved to be loathsome and those we have revered to be disreputable, even despicable.[4]

To understand how a system of higher education that was originally built on a foundation of Christian principles could have retreated so far from these principles, one must begin at the beginning. Consequently, this chapter provides an overview of the origins of higher education in America by relating the founding stories of several of our nation's oldest and most widely-recognized universities. The institutions profiled are known worldwide and revered by many, but without exception they have strayed far from their Christian roots. In order of longevity the institutions profiled are: Harvard, William and Mary, Yale, Princeton, Columbia, Brown, Rutgers, and Dartmouth.

HARVARD UNIVERSITY (1636): PURITAN CONGREGATIONAL AFFILIATION

Founded in 1636, Harvard is the oldest university in the United States. Located in Cambridge, Massachusetts, the school is named after an early benefactor, John Harvard, a minister who bequeathed his library and half of his estate to the institution. This turned out to be the beginning of an endowment that is now approaching $30 billion.

Harvard's original mission was to train ministers. John Winthrop's description of the institution's founding leaves no room for doubt concerning Harvard's Christian roots.

> After God had carried us safe to New England, and we had built our houses, provided necessaries for our livelihood, reared convenient places for God's worship, and led the civil government, one of the next things we longed for and looked after was to advance learning and perpetuate it to posterity; dreading to leave an illiterate ministry to the churches, when our present ministers shall lie in the dust. And as we were thinking and consulting how to perfect this great work, it pleased God to stir up the heart of one Mr. Harvard (a godly gentlemen and a lover of learning, there living among us) to give one-half of his estate (it being in all about £700) toward the founding of a college, and all of his library...Over the college is Master Dunster placed as president, a learned, a conscionable, and industrious man, who has so trained up his pupils in the tongues and arts, and so seasoned them with the principles of divinity and Christianity, that we have to our great comfort (and in truth) beyond our hopes, beheld their progress in learning and godliness also.[5]

Most of Harvard's early graduates became Christian ministers in Puritan churches. The college's motto for many years was "Veritas Christo et Ecclesiae" which is Latin for "Truth in Christ and the Church." It has since been shortened to just "Veritas" or "Truth." An early directive to Harvard's students summarized the purpose of their education: "Let every student be plainly instructed and consider well that the main end of his life and studies is to know God and Jesus, which is eternal life. And therefore to lay Christ at the bottom as the only foundation of all sound learning and knowledge."[6]

THE COLLEGE OF WILLIAM AND MARY (1693): ANGLICAN AFFILIATION

William and Mary—although a university—still uses its original name, *The College of William and Mary.* The school was founded in 1693 and is located in Williamsburg, Virginia. It is named after King William III and Queen Mary II who were the reigning monarchs of Great Britain at the time of the school's founding. The founder and first president of William and Mary, Dr. James Blair, was a Scottish clergyman in the Anglican Church. His original assignment in the colony of Virginia was to revive and reform the Anglican Church there. Part of his plan for doing this was to establish a college that would supply well-educated ministers for the colony. This purpose is made clear in the original act of the Virginia Assembly establishing the college where it says that the college would supply the Church in Virginia "with a seminary of ministers" so that the "Christian Faith may be propagated amongst the Western Indians, to the Glory of Almighty God."[7]

YALE UNIVERSITY (1701): CONGREGATIONAL AFFILIATION

Yale was founded as the Collegiate School of Connecticut in 1701 by ten Congregationalist ministers. These ministers, known as the "Founders," each donated books from their personal libraries to form the school's first library.   Originally located in Killingworth, Connecticut, Yale moved to its present location in New Haven in 1716. The traditional rivalry between Yale and Harvard began early in the school's history. The sixth president of Harvard, Increase Mather (1639–1723), was growing increasingly disenchanted with what he saw as the liberal views of Harvard's faculty. Mather was a Puritan minister and a leading figure in the development of the Massachusetts Bay Colony. Mather thought Harvard's faculty members were becoming lax in terms of both ecclesiastics and church polity. Unable to win the feud, Mather resigned as president of Harvard and attempted to convince the administration to hire his son, Cotton Mather, as his successor. Cotton Mather (1663–1728)—a Puritan minister, historian, pioneer in the field of science, and prolific writer—was certainly qualified. However, the Harvard faculty had tired of the Mathers. When it became clear that Cotton Mather would never be president of Harvard, father and son joined in supporting the development of the Collegiate School of Connecticut. Their hope was that this budding college would adhere more closely to Puritan religious orthodoxy than had Harvard.[8]

Cotton Mather was even partially responsible for the new college eventually adopting the name of "Yale." In 1718, Mather contacted a businessman from Wales named Elihu Yale and asked for his financial assistance in building a new facility for the Collegiate School. Yale responded favorably by donating both money and books. Mather suggested the school show its gratitude by changing its name to Yale, which it did.[9] The first name of the University's namesake—Elihu—is why a Yale graduate is referred to as an "Eli."

PRINCETON UNIVERSITY (1746):
PRESBYTERIAN AFFILIATION

Princeton University, which is now located in Princeton, New Jersey was founded in 1746, but is an indirect descendant of an early institution founded in Pennsylvania in 1726 known as the "Log College." The Log College was founded by Presbyterian minister William Tennet. Its graduates played leading roles in spreading the Great Awakening—an 18th century religious movement marked by zealous revivals. In New England, the activities of some revivalists led to dissension within churches and eventually caused splits. Most prominently, in the years 1741 to 1758, the Presbyterian Church underwent a split known as the Great Schism in which members divided themselves into two opposing camps—the "New Sides" and the "Old Sides." This split indirectly led to the establishment of Princeton.[10]

Unhappy with what they saw as a limited curriculum at the Log College and disenchanted with both Harvard and Yale for failing to support the Great Awakening, four moderate "New Side" ministers decided to start a new college in New Jersey, which was considered a middle colony. Late in 1745 the founders petitioned Governor Lewis Morris, an Anglican, for a charter but he refused. However, following his death, the acting governor, John Hamilton—also an Anglican— granted the charter in 1746. The Anglican Church, unhappy with Hamilton for granting the charter to members of the Presbyterian Church, threatened to challenge its validity in court. However, this effort was preempted when a new governor, Jonathan Belcher—a Congregationalist—issued a second charter in September 1748. Original members of the college's board of trustees included Presbyterians, members of the Society of Friends (Quakers), Episcopalians, and a member of the Dutch Reformed Church.[11]

COLUMBIA UNIVERSITY (1754): ANGLICAN AFFILIATION

Columbia University in New York City was established as King's College in 1754 by a royal charter of King George II of England. Columbia's roots are in the Anglican Church and its first classes were taught in the Trinity Church schoolhouse. The school's location in New York City has changed several times, and today one would have to look hard to find even the faintest vestiges of its Christian roots. However, the school's original shield—adopted in 1755—makes clear the worldviews of Columbia's founders:

> Over the head of the seated woman is the (Hebrew) Tetragrammaton, YHVH (*Jehovah*); the Latin around her head means "In Thy light we see light" (Psalm 36:10); the Hebrew phrase on the ribbon is *Uri El* ("God is my light"), an allusion to Psalm 27:1; and at the feet of the woman is the New Testament passage commanding Christians to desire the pure milk of God's word (1 Peter 2:1-2). The only line remaining from the original shield is the Latin phrase "In Thy light we see light."[12]

BROWN UNIVERSITY (1764): BAPTIST AFFILIATION

Brown University, located in Providence, Rhode Island, was founded in 1764 primarily through the work of James Manning, a Baptist minister, and a group of Congregationalists. Brown's motto is "In Deo speramus" which is Latin for "In God we hope." The founding charter for the university required that its board of trustees include 22 Baptists, five Friends (Quakers), four Congregationalists, and five Episcopalians. It also specified that the president be Baptist. James Manning, the principal founder of Brown, became its first president. In keeping with its original charter to focus on arts and sciences, Brown has an engineering school but no school of business or law.[13]

RUTGERS UNIVERSITY (1766):
DUTCH REFORMED AFFILIATION

Rutgers University was founded in 1766 as Queen's College by ministers of the Dutch Reformed Church who were seeking greater autonomy in ecclesiastical affairs. Its original purpose was to prepare ministers for service in the American colonies and to "educate the youth in language, the divinity, and useful arts and sciences"[14] The founders of Rutgers were Reverends Theodorus Jacobus Frelinghuysen and Jacob Rutsen Hardenbergh. Reverend Hardenbergh became the college's first president. The university's motto is "Sol Iustitiae et Occidentem Illustra" which is Latin for "Sun of righteousness, shine upon the West also."[15]

DARTMOUTH COLLEGE (1769):
PURITAN AFFILIATION

Dartmouth College, located in Hanover, New Hampshire, was founded in 1769. Although it is a university, Dartmouth chooses to use its original name "The Trustees of Dartmouth College" or just "Dartmouth College." The college was founded by Puritan minister Eleazar Wheelock with the assistance of Samson Occom, an American Indian preacher. The school's motto is "Vox clamantis in deserto" which is Latin for "The voice of one crying out in the wilderness" (a reference to John the Baptist). Dartmouth's original purpose was to provide for the Christianization, instruction, and education of the "Youth of Indian Tribes in this land...and also of English Youth and any others."[16]

As these brief summaries of America's first colleges show, the historical record is clear concerning the Christian heritage of higher education in this country. Unfortunately, it is a heritage that for the most part is now denied by left-leaning revisionists in many of America's major universities. The founders of America's first colleges would neither recognize nor appreciate what their institutions have become.

America's earliest colleges reflected the values of the society they served: Christian values. This is as it should be. In order to serve society, universities must be in touch with society. Unfortunately, in a time when the left dominates so many university campuses, this is typically not the case. Today, many universities are not just out of touch with the values of American society, they are completely at odds with them; which, of course, is why they work so hard to undermine them. Universities give a great deal of lip service to tolerance, but in actual practice they are increasingly intolerant of views that lack the radical left's seal of approval, views such as Christianity and conservatism.

Increasingly, left-leaning faculty members advocate worldviews that are openly hostile to Christian and conservative values. The faculties in many of America's major universities have become self-validating, self-perpetuating enclaves of leftist thinking, isolated and insulated from the very society they purport to serve. This fact threatens the future of higher education in this country and, in turn, of the country itself, because the futures of the two are inextricably linked, and because secular humanism is opposed to our civilization and destructive in its consequences.

In too many cases, leftist college professors appear more concerned with teaching students *what* to think than *how* to think. As these liberal professors gain control of the faculties in more and more universities, this tyranny is becoming majority tyranny: suppression of the rights and liberties of the minority by the majority; the minority in this case being professors and students who have Christian and conservative worldviews. Teaching people how to think is called education. Teaching them what to think is called indoctrination. When indoctrination is allowed to supplant education in the halls of the academy, universities have started down the path to disaster.

EXPELLING GOD FROM COLLEGE

The sinful nature of man is such that America's first institutions of higher education wasted little time in beginning their retreat from Christian values. However, as is often the case with such situations, progress toward the secularization of higher education was originally slow and incremental. The *boiling-the-frog syndrome* has always been a favored tactic of anti-Christian movements.

The movement to expel God from college picked up steam in America following World War II and really gained traction during the turbulent 1960s. As a result, the radical left has made great strides toward its goal of dominating university faculties. Without question, the left understands that in order to control the hearts, minds, and values of future generations, they must first control the faculties of flagship universities—those that set the trends and provide the leadership for other institutions of higher education. Even a cursory look at what is happening on the campuses of America's major universities will show that the left has not only made progress, but is winning the battle. Not only does God no longer have a seat in the classroom, He has been expelled from college.

Heroes of the Radical Left

According to Dinesh D'Souza, author of *Illiberal Education: The Politics of Race and Sex on Campus*,

> In recent years there has arisen a new atheism that represents a direct attack on Western Christianity. Books such as Richard Dawkins' *The God Delusion*, Christopher Hitchens' *God Is Not Great*, and Sam Harris' *The End of Faith*, all contend that Western society would be better off if we could eradicate from it the last vestiges of Christianity.[17]

The fact that all of these books are best sellers shows just how effective the radical left has been in reshaping the worldviews of many Americans. The authors of these attacks on Christianity have become some of the most esteemed heroes of the radical left.

After undermining the sanctity of the family and the quality of America's public schools, one of the more effective strategies of the radical left has been to redefine the concept of the "hero." When the first colleges were established in America, most heroes were biblical characters. Later, George Washington and the other founding fathers were added to America's honor roll of most admired. But the radical left, aided by the media, has turned the concept of the hero upside down. It is no longer the men and women who built America who are admired, but those who are bent on tearing it down, people such as Dawkins, Hitchens, Harris, and other leaders of the radical left. The irony of ironies in this situation is that radical leftists use the very freedoms afforded them *by* America as a protective shield when making their attacks *on* America.

One can learn a good deal about a community by studying its heroes, including the academic community. Therefore, it is worthwhile in the current context to contrast these modern-day "heroes" of the radical left with the authentic heroes they have supplanted. A quick look at the views of Dawkins, Hitchens, and Harris is instructive in this regard.

Richard Dawkins is an atheist, biologist, and professorial fellow of New College, Oxford. He also holds the Charles Simonyi Chair for the Public Understanding of Science at the University of Oxford. But he is best known as author of *The God Delusion*. In this bestselling book, Dawkins contends

> that a supernatural creator does not exist and that belief in a personal god qualifies as a delusion, which he defines as a persistent false belief held in the face of strong contradictory evidence.[18]

Dawkins seems oblivious to the fact that this statement applies directly to his own anti-God worldview. He is a hugely popular speaker on college campuses and is often quoted with great relish and appreciation by the radical left. One of his frequently quoted statements is:

> Faith is the great cop-out, the great excuse to evade the
> need to think and evaluate evidence. Faith is belief in spite
> of, even perhaps because of, the lack of evidence.[19]

Christopher Hitchens, although not an academician like Dawkins, is widely admired in the halls of the academy. He is an anti-theist rather than an atheist. Hitchens is an ardent advocate of the values of secularism, humanism, and rationalism (faith in man's supposedly self-sufficient ability to reason). His book, *God Is Not Great: How Religion Poisons Everything*, made him a widely sought speaker on talk shows and college campuses. In this book, Hitchens attacks not just Christianity but all religions—although he reserves his most vitriolic diatribes for Judaism, Christianity, and Islam; which Hitchens calls "the three great monotheisms."[20]

Hitchens does well in front of supportive liberal audiences, but appears less sure of himself in debates with informed scholars who do not share his anti-religion message; a common pattern observable in leftist thinkers. This is, no doubt, one of the reasons leftist professors so often choose to suppress Christian and conservative points of view (rather than allow them to be heard.) Many liberals have learned the hard way that kicking against the brick wall of truth only gives one a sore foot; it is much easier to just suppress it.

Sam Harris is an atheist, non-fiction writer, and philosopher. The underlying theme of his books and lectures is that religion threatens the survival of civilization—a ridiculous thesis given the foundational role that religion has played in the advancement of civilization. He was propelled into prominence by his book, *The End of Faith*. The underlying theme of this book is that religion is the only field of endeavor which can offer no evidence to support its conclusions and beliefs; an argument which, at best, reveals an astounding ignorance of Christian apologetics.[21] One of Harris' often-quoted statements is:

> The idea, therefore, that religious faith is somehow a
> *sacred* human convention—distinguished, as it is, both

by the extravagance of its claims and by the paucity of its evidence—is really too great a monstrosity to be appreciated in all its glory. Religious faith represents so uncompromising a misuse of the power of our minds that it forms a kind of perverse, cultural singularity— a vanishing point beyond which rational discourse proves impossible.[22]

False Gods on Campus

It is not religion but Christianity that has been supplanted on the campuses of left-leaning universities. Today's radical left professors are just as religious as were their academic ancestors who founded higher education in America. The difference is that the radical left worships at the altar of secular humanism, rather than at the feet of God. Their relativistic religion is not just man-centered, it is "me"-centered. Consequently, the ultimate god of the left is not just the individual, it is the specific individual who happens to have power, control, or influence in a given situation. This is a convenient worldview if you wish to be the ultimate authority concerning right and wrong, which is precisely what the radical left in America's universities wants.

Moral relativists reject Christ and the apostles while deifying the ancient Greek and Roman philosophers. Studying Aristotle, Anaximenes, Diogenes, Heraclitus, Plato, Socrates, Xenophon and the other giants of the ancient Greek and Roman worlds is certainly a worthy undertaking and should be part of the college experience, but elevating them to the level of deity is overdoing it. Christian scholars also study the Greek and Roman philosophers and acknowledge their contributions, but unlike their leftist colleagues, Christian scholars do not deify them or turn them into saints. Rather, they know that Plato, Aristotle, Socrates, and other thinkers of the ancient world had feet of clay—as all men do. Moreover, they know the religious and philosophical failures of the views of these ancient man-centered thinkers.

In fact, as Dinesh D'Souza accurately points out, freedom in the ancient world of the Greeks and Romans, who are so admired by left-leaning professors, really meant the freedom to make the laws. Ancient

Greek and Roman leaders understood that he who makes the rules, rules. This is why the radical left has worked so hard to gain the upper hand in university faculties. If they can dominate academic departments, they can determine who receives tenure and who does not, the content of courses, the books to be used when teaching courses, how controversial and unsettled social, ethical, economic, and political issues are handled, and—most important of all—how the concept of academic freedom is interpreted and applied.

ACADEMIC FREEDOM: PROTECTOR OF FREE THOUGHT OR INSTRUMENT OF SUPPRESSION?

Academic freedom is a nebulous concept that is widely misunderstood and increasingly abused by liberal faculties. The first thing that should be understood about academic freedom is that it is an academic tradition, not a Constitutional guarantee. Nonetheless, if properly interpreted and applied, it can be a useful protector of free thought. However, if misused by a majority determined to maintain control and advance a specific agenda, it can be an effective instrument of suppression. Here is what the American Federation of Teachers says about the concept of academic freedom:

> Faculty and professional staff must be able to exercise independent academic judgment in the conduct of their teaching and research. Academic freedom is important because society needs "safe havens," places where students and scholars can challenge the conventional wisdom of any field—art, science, politics or whatever. This is not a threat to society; it strengthens society. It puts ideas to the test and teaches students to think and defend their ideas.[23]

This is a good definition. Universities should be "safe havens" for discussion and the reasoned debate of diverse ideas. Students and faculty should be allowed and even encouraged to challenge conventional wisdom in any field. This ideal, if actually realized, can strengthen society. Further, putting ideas to the test can, in fact, teach students to think and sharpen their skills at defending their worldviews. This is a skill Christians who study apologetics hope to develop. But where the concept of academic freedom breaks down is in its application.

If scholars should be encouraged to "challenge the conventional wisdom of any field," why are those who challenge the conventions of Darwinism being demonized, shunned, denied tenure, and even fired? If universities truly want to teach students how to think and defend their ideas in reasoned debate, why do they allow leftist professors to browbeat students who advocate Christian and conservative views? It is abuses such as these that undermine what could and should be a valid, helpful concept. Part of the tyranny of leftist faculties is their determination to apply academic freedom in such a way that it really means the freedom to agree with them.

Academic Bill of Rights

Abuse of any kind will eventually result in an *enough-is-enough* response, which is what has happened in the case of academic freedom. Majority tyranny on the part of leftist faculties has led to the establishment of Students for Academic Freedom, a spinoff group of the David Horowitz Freedom Center (formerly the Center for the Study of Popular Culture). Students for Academic Freedom, in turn, developed an Academic Bill of Rights for the express purpose of ending "the political abuse of the university and to restore integrity to the academic mission as a disinterested pursuit of knowledge."[24] The Bill contains eight principles designed to create an academic environment in which decisions are not biased by one's personal, political, or religious beliefs. These principles can be summarized as follows:

- All faculty members shall be hired, fired, promoted and granted tenure on the basis of their competence and appropriate knowledge in their fields of expertise. Plurality should be fostered in the humanities, social sciences, and arts. Political and religious beliefs should not affect hiring, firing, promotion, and tenure decisions.

- Faculty members shall not be excluded from the decision-making process for granting tenure on the basis of their religious or political beliefs.

- Students should be graded solely on the basis of their reasoned answers and knowledge of their studies and not on the basis of political or religious beliefs.

- Curricula and reading lists in the humanities and social sciences should provide students with dissenting viewpoints where appropriate. While teachers should be free to pursue their own findings and points of view, they should make their students aware of other points of view. Diversity of thought should be welcomed.

- Faculty members are responsible for exposing students to a wide range of scholarly viewpoints. They should not use their courses for the purpose of indoctrination.

- The process for selecting speakers and allocating funds to pay them should observe the principles of academic freedom and intellectual pluralism.

- An environment conducive to the civil exchange of ideas should be maintained. Attempts to obstruct the civil exchange of ideas should not be tolerated.

- Academic institutions and professional societies should maintain a stance of organizational neutrality concerning the substantive disagreements of researchers within and outside of their fields of inquiry.[25]

The Academic Bill of Rights is not a perfect document. However, it is a legitimate attempt to rectify an intolerable situation in higher education. Although there are a few conservative and libertarian critics who associate it with over-regulation and speech codes, most of the criticism of the Bill comes from the left and includes such organizations as the American Association of University Professors, American Library Association, American Federation of Teachers, Refuse and Resist, the AFL-CIO, and SourceWatch. The criticism emanating from these groups amounts to little more than left-leaning organizations attempting to preserve their domination of the system.

The American Association of University Professors, for example, claims that the Bill "infringes academic freedom in the very act of purporting to protect it."[26] The irony in this statement is that it summarizes succinctly what leftist faculties are doing in the name of academic freedom in universities across the country. If academic freedom were being used as a tool to protect free thought rather than an instrument for suppressing it, there would be no need for an Academic Bill of Rights. The Bill is an example of an *enough-is-enough* response to leftist suppression of Christian and conservative thought. Consequently, leftist critics of the Bill have no one to blame but themselves when initiatives such as this gain traction with students, parents, and the taxpaying public.

Universities in America were established by Christians as Christian enterprises, but over time many have devolved to the point that Christian and conservative points of view are no longer welcome. The faculties of many institutions of higher education are out of touch with American society. As a result, many Americans are saying "enough is enough." This book was written to help these Americans understand how they can fight back and, in the process, rescue America's colleges and universities from the excesses of liberal tyranny.

LIBERAL DOMINATION OF UNIVERSITY FACULTIES

In his book, *Illiberal Education: The Politics of Race and Sex on Campus,* Dinesh D'Souza quotes Abigail Thernstrom's view of today's flagship universities in America, which she calls "islands of repression in a sea of freedom."[27] Conservative critic David Horowitz claims that students are deprived of a decent education because left-leaning professors have a monopoly on the faculties of universities.[28] Are university faculties really dominated by liberal professors? This question is answered conclusively in a study conducted by Bruce L.R. Smith, Jeremy D. Mayer, and A. Lee Fritschler, and the findings are published in a book they wrote based on the study.[29] What follows are pertinent findings from their research:

- Professors who identify themselves as liberal outnumber conservatives by a ratio of 3:1.

- There has been an increase in the number of professors who identify with the left when compared with the 1960s and 1970s.

- When asked how they describe themselves ideologically, almost 61 percent of university professors say either "strongly liberal" or "moderately liberal."

- Professors in the hard sciences are now even more liberal than their colleagues in the social sciences.

- The most liberal departments are English, foreign languages, sociology, history, physics, and religious studies.

- The ratio of professors who are Democrats versus Republicans is 4:1.

- When asked to describe their perceptions of the political views of their colleagues, 61 percent of professors chose either "strongly" or "moderately" liberal.

- Conservative professors express discontent with the current campus environment as it relates to politics.

- When asked if professors are more liberal than their students, 59 percent said they were.

- When asked if their colleagues ever grade unfairly on the basis of political views, 53 percent claimed it happens either "occasionally" or "often." When bias is shown on the basis of political views, 31 percent thought it is liberal bias against conservative views.

Based on the findings of the research conducted by Smith, Mayer, and Fritschler, one could reasonably ask: "Can a university that purports to advocate free speech, thought, and inquiry as fundamental to providing a well-rounded education for students really live up to this ideal when its faculty's worldviews are so skewed to the left?" How can students hope to acquaint themselves with a broad spectrum of views when the professors who guide their studies are likely to be liberal by a three-to-one margin? How can advocates of such concepts as intelligent design hope to get a fair and impartial hearing for their research findings when professors in the hard sciences are even more liberal than their social science colleagues?

How can Christian and conservative students hope to express their points of view in an atmosphere of encouragement and support when professors who are Democrats outnumber Republicans by a ratio of four to one? How can Christian and conservative students hope to participate fully in the marketplace of ideas when 59 percent of their professors are more liberal than their students? Finally, how can Christian and conservative students hope to make the top grades necessary for admission to graduate school or to be competitive in the job market when 53 percent of professors claim that there is bias in grading based on political views?

Confessions of a Liberal

In a refreshingly open, frank, and honest article, Gowri Krishna of Washington University in St. Louis, tells how her liberal upbringing and education misled her to believe that she and those who believed like her were the font of all wisdom when it came to determining right and wrong and that Republicans represented the "dark side."[30] She received a "slap in the face" when she took a summer position in the office of Republican Senator, Richard Lugar, something she did with much trepidation. Krishna had been conditioned to fear that she would be brainwashed and persuaded—heaven forbid—to vote for George W. Bush. Predictably, at least for anyone not conditioned to view non-liberals as members of the "dark side," Krishna's experience was much different than what she expected it to be.[31] She writes:

Imagine your pre-conceived notions having no sub-
stance; imagine not knowing the immediate answer to
problems; imagine being able to see more than two sides
to an issue ... this seemed a revelation. A slap-in-the-
face revelation ... Within five weeks of my internship,
I even began thinking that perhaps George W. Bush in
office would not be so bad (this coming from the same
person who swore she would leave the country if such a
thing occurred) ... The hardest part of meeting the Gray
is remembering that it exists. It is very easy to slip back
into the mode where everything is black and white or
somehow stereotypical...However, we must make the effort to see life's intricacies and to respect them. While
a summer in the Gray was, at times, confusing, I stand
witness to the fact that one will be able to survive such
an experience; that in fact, one will emerge with a greater appreciation for difference. [32]

What Krishna said in this article—without actually stating it—is that
after many years of indoctrination by liberal parents, teachers, and
professors, she finally received an education in the office of a Republican Senator. Her eyes were opened in less than ten weeks. She does not
claim to have undergone a conversion experience. In fact, she appears
to have retained her democratic and liberal worldview. However, she
does now recognize that others may have valid opinions and worldviews and she is open to hearing them. If a self-proclaimed liberal
Democrat can make this much progress in just ten weeks, imagine
what would happen if Christian and conservative views were given
opportunities to be openly professed, discussed, and debated over the
course of an entire education. But, of course, that is precisely what
left-leaning professors fear.

Clearly, many of the major universities in America have strayed far
from their roots and veered off-track concerning the pursuit of their
overall mission. The current situation does not bode well for Christian
and conservative students much less their parents, who hoped to see
them receive an education that would make them competitive in the

global marketplace. When students with Christian and conservative worldviews cannot receive a college education without selling their souls or checking their ethical, social, or political views at the door, something is drastically wrong. That something is the liberal tyranny that is taking place on university campuses nationwide.

NOTES

1. Gary DeMar, *America's Christian History: The Untold Story* (Atlanta, GA: American Vision, 2008), 9.

2. Ari Goldman, *The Search for God at Harvard* (New York: Ballantine Books, 1992), 16.

3. George Orwell, *1984* (New York: Signet Classics, 1961), 32.

4. Patrick J. Buchanan, *The Death of the West* (New York: Thomas Dunne Books, an imprint of St. Martin's Press, 2002), 148.

5. Quoted in "Harvard University's Founding Vision and Mission—A Timely Reminder." Retrieved from http://www.albertmohler.com/blog_read.php?id=519 on January 9, 2009.

6. "Harvard University History." Retrieved from www.ivysport.com/category-category_id/334 on January 9, 2009.

7. "Charter of William and Mary," in Cohen, *Education in the United States,* 2:645.

8. "Yale University History." Retrieved from www.ivysport.com/category-category_id/337 on January 9, 2009.

9. "Yale University History."

10. "The Founding of Princeton." Retrieved from http://etcweb.princeton.edu/CampusWWW/Companion/founding_princeton.html on June 9, 2009.

11. "The Founding of Princeton."

12. DeMar, *America's Christian History*, 106-107.

13. "Brown University History." Retrieved from www.ivysport.com/category-category_id/330 on January 12, 2009.

14. "Rutgers University." Retrieved from http://www.Rutgers.edu on May 8, 2009.

15. "Rutgers University."

16. "Dartmouth College History." Retrieved from http://www.ivysport.com/category-category_id/333 on January 12, 2009.

17. Dinesh D'Souza, "Created Equal: How Christianity Shaped the West," *Imprimis* (Vol. 37, No. 11), November 2008, 1.

18. Richard Dawkins, *The God Delusion*, (Boston: Houghton-Mifflin, 2006).

19. "Richard Dawkins: Quotes and Excerpts." Retrieved from http://www.simonyi.ox.ac. uk/dawkins/WorldOfDawkins-archive/Catalano/quotes.shtml on January 13, 2009.

20. Christopher Hitchens, *God is Not Great: How Religion Poisons Everything*, (New York: Twelve, 2007).

21. "Sam Harris, *The End of Faith: Religion, Terror, and the Future of Reason*, (New York: W.W. Norton, 2005), 72.

22. Harris, *The End of Faith*, 63.

23. "Academic Freedom in Higher Education." Retrieved from http://www.aft.org/topics/ academic-freedom/on January 15, 2009.

24. "Academic Bill of Rights." Retrieved from www.taup.org/taupweb2006/hr177/aborhorowitz. pdf on May 8, 2009.

25. "Academic Bill of Rights."

26. "Academic Bill of Rights."

27. As quoted in Dinesh D'Souza, *Illiberal Education: The Politics of Race and Sex on Campus* (New York: Free Press, 1991), 227.

28. Patrick Coyle and Ron Robinson, *The Conservative Guide to Campus Activism* (Herndon, VA: Young Americans Foundation, 2005), 5.

29. Bruce L. R. Smith, Jeremy D. Mayer, and A. Lee Fritschler, *Closed Minds? Politics and Ideology in American Universities* (Washington, DC: Brookings Institution Press, 2008).

30. Gowri Krishna, "Summer in the Gray: Politics, Stereotypes, and a Slap in the Face," *NASPA Journal of College and Character*. Retrieved from http://collegevalues.org/reflec- tions.cfm?id=291&a=1 on January 21, 2009.

31. Krishna, "Summer in the Gray."

32. Krishna, "Summer in the Gray."

Three

Secular Humanism: The Religion of the Left

"From a knowledge of his work, we shall know him."
—Robert Boyle

Freedom *from* religion is a fundamental tenet of secular humanism. The left's interpretation of the First Amendment is that it requires a forced segregation of religion from all aspects of public life. This is both a disingenuous and hypocritical interpretation. The disingenuous aspect is that the left knowingly and purposefully misinterprets the "Free Exercise" and "Establishment" clauses of the First Amendment which say: "Congress shall make no law respecting an establishment of religion, or prohibiting the free exercise thereof." Beyond choosing to ignore the historical fact that our founders intended this language to protect against the type of state-supported established church they had fled England to avoid, their interpretation is disingenuous because it focuses on the first clause and ignores the second.

The hypocritical aspect of the left's interpretation of the First Amendment is that they are not really opposed to religion *per se*, just the Christian religion. In fact, they typically bend over backwards to accommodate Islam, Hinduism, and Buddhism on campus. Further, liberals are just as religious as Christians; the difference is found in whom and what they worship. While Christians worship the omniscient, never-changing Creator and ruler of the universe, secular humanists worship a limited and ever-changing god: man. The religion of the left is secular humanism.

Because, as Christians, God is our authority, we believe in right and wrong and look to the Bible for guidance in distinguishing between the two. God's specific revelation concerning who He is, who we are, and how we should live is found in Holy Scripture. Hence, regardless of denomination, the Bible provides a common starting point for helping Christians make determinations about right and wrong.

Putting aside for the moment the fact that God is the ultimate authority concerning right and wrong, whether liberals wish to admit it or not, it is important to have a common starting point when discussing and debating such matters. Consider what happens when two people try to settle an issue of right and wrong but lack a common basis for deciding. They are like two surveyors trying to settle a property claim who start their work from two different points of beginning. The claim will never be settled. The only way one survey can either validate or refute another is if the surveyors start at a common point of beginning. The lesson in this analogy is one that secular humanists choose to ignore. Those who do not wish to be bound by the moral constraints of Christianity must find an alternative. That alternative, at least for the left, is secular humanism. While Christians look to the Bible and the example of Christ for guidance in matters of right and wrong, secular humanists rely on the concept of moral relativism.

MORAL RELATIVISM DEFINED

Moral relativism is a fundamental tenet of the secular humanist's worldview. It claims right and wrong are culturally-based and man-made, thus they are subject to the determination of the individual. If God decides right and wrong and man is god, then man decides right and wrong. In layman's terms, moral relativism means that there are no absolutes; each individual can decide for himself what is right and what is wrong.

Secular humanists believe in the evolutionary view that life on earth is the result of countless cosmic accidents. This being the case, life is accidental and therefore lacks any meaning more substantive than whatever makes a given individual happy at the moment. Consequently, anything the individual chooses to do is acceptable because in the long run it is not going to matter anyway. From the convenient perspective of moral relativism, if something is right for me, it is right period. This is an attractive point of view for those who feel constrained by the Judeo-Christian ethic. In adopting moral relativism as part of their worldview, secular humanists are applying a strategy that is as old as mankind itself: If the rules get in the way of what you want, make new rules.

IS MORAL RELATIVISM REALLY MORALLY NEUTRAL?

Secular humanists like to claim that moral relativism—you do your thing and I'll do mine—is a morally neutral concept. This, of course, is a practical impossibility—nothing is morally neutral. In an article entitled, "Moral Relativism – Neutral Thinking," the president of Planned Parenthood is quoted as saying: "teaching morality doesn't mean imposing my moral values on others. It means sharing wisdom, giving reasons for believing as I do—and then trusting others to think and judge for themselves."[1] Even a cursory reading of this statement reveals the absurdity of the claim of moral neutrality. The only reason for making such a statement is to influence the thinking of others. Hence, the arguments for moral relativism are, by their very nature, self-defeating.

Secular humanists who argue for moral relativism argue against themselves. For example, tell a proponent of moral relativism that you advocate child abuse and you are likely to be reported to government authorities. However, if the secular humanist who reports you really believes that right and wrong are matters of individual choice, how can he argue against child abuse? After all, there are certainly individuals—many of them—who choose to abuse children.

Because of this inherent flaw in their philosophy, secular humanists have taken to adding a disclaimer to their arguments for moral relativism. They now say that whatever the individual believes is right, unless it hurts someone else. But, of course, the disclaimer is as flawed as the concept. If everything is relative, it cannot be wrong to hurt someone else. If it is wrong to hurt someone else, why then do liberal professors who worship at the altar of moral relativism participate in denying tenure to or even firing proponents of intelligent design?

Such actions, by their own definition, must be wrong. After all, they certainly hurt the professors who are the victims. How do moral relativists justify supporting abortion when the child whose life is taken is certainly hurt—as is the mother, whether she realizes it or not—not to mention society in general? There is no end to these types of questions, and no acceptable answer from proponents of moral relativism. Logic is not on the side of secular humanism.

Obviously, moral relativism is a flawed concept. None the less, it is considered sacred ground among leftist members of the academy. For example, a Zogby poll shows that 75 percent of college professors teach that there is no such thing as right and wrong, that good and evil are relative concepts based on individual and cultural interpretation.[2] Yet, these same professors are quick to claim that Christian and conservative worldviews are wrong. Consider what Robert Brandon, professor of biology and philosophy at Duke University, had to say when questioned about liberal bias at his institution: "If, as John Stuart Mill said, stupid people are generally conservative, then there are lots of conservatives we will never hire.... Members of academia tend to be a bit smarter than average."[3]

William McGuffey, author of the classic elementary readers used to teach generations of Americans, said: "Erase all thought and fear of God from a community, and selfishness and sensuality would absorb the whole man."[4] This is a prophetic statement because it provides an accurate description of what is happening on university campuses throughout America, as a by-product of secular humanism and its subset, moral relativism.

HUMANIST MANIFESTO: THE BIBLE FOR SECULAR HUMANISTS/MORAL RELATIVISTS

Like most religions, secular humanism has a "bible." Liberals look to the *Humanist Manifesto* as their sacred book. There are actually three versions of the *Manifesto*: 1) the original *Humanist Manifesto* published in 1933 (*Humanist Manifesto I*), 2) *Humanist Manifesto II* published in 1973, and 3) *Humanism and Its Aspirations* published in 2003 (*Humanist Manifesto III*). All three of these books describe a worldview absent of God or any other kind of higher power. The God of humanism is man. All three versions of the *Manifesto* have been signed by prominent left-leaning members of the academy, but not without some controversy.

The *Manifesto* has been updated and revised over time as humanist thinking has ebbed and flowed, and as disagreements among proponents of secular humanism have emerged as a result. The fickle nature of man is just one of many factors that undermines the fundamental validity of a man-centered religion. Consequently, each successive version of the *Manifesto* has sought to correct the perceived weaknesses of its predecessor and answer criticisms from both the right and left.

Humanist Manifesto I

The original *Manifesto* was written in 1933. It presented a new belief system to replace religions founded on supernatural revelation. The new belief system it proposed amounted to an egalitarian worldview based on voluntary mutual cooperation among all people; an ideal rendered impossible from the outset by the sinful nature of man. Predictably, there was disagreement about various aspects of the *Manifesto* among those involved in developing it, a circumstance inherent in all human endeavors. Consequently, the originally proposed title, "The Humanist Manifesto," had to be changed to "A Humanist Manifesto."

Ironically, the original *Manifesto* contained a basic tenet that now haunts, embarrasses, and even angers modern-day liberals. It referred to humanism as a religion; something today's liberals go to great lengths to deny since freedom FROM religion is the cornerstone of their man-centered worldview. If secular humanists admit that their views of morality are a religion, the hypocrisy of their efforts to ban religion from the classroom, public square, and marketplace of ideas is exposed. When this happens, the left will be forced to admit that Christianity is their real target—not religion—something even a casual observer of the American culture wars already knows.

Humanist Manifesto II

The horrors of World War II, perpetrated by the followers of Hitler and Stalin in Europe, not to mention those of Tojo in Japan, exploded the ideal that was at the heart of the original *Manifesto*. With the evidence of Hitler's death camps, Stalin's pogroms, and Tojo's rape of Nanking revealed to the world, even the most idealistic of humanists had to admit that their hope for a worldwide egalitarian society based on voluntary mutual cooperation might have been a little too optimistic. One can only wonder why the horrors of World War II did not lead humanists to abandon their intellectual and moral relativism.

Admitting the naiveté of the first document, drafters of the revised *Manifesto* took a more realistic approach. Rather than pursuing a worldwide egalitarian society based on voluntary mutual cooperation, the drafters of *Manifesto II* set more "realistic" goals, including the elimination of war and poverty. Of course, if intellectual and moral relativism were valid concepts, there would be nothing wrong with war and no reason to eliminate poverty. None of the document's authors or supporters thought to ask how these goals could be achieved without changing the heart of man. If man is god, why try to change his heart? When one will not admit that man has a sinful nature, it is easy to naively think that war and hunger can be eliminated by simply displaying heart-tugging bumper stickers on your car. Surely, slogans such as "Give Peace a Chance"—if displayed on enough bumpers—will end war.

One of the most controversial and frequently quoted verses from *Manifesto II* is: "Humans are responsible for what we are or will become. No deity will save us; we must save ourselves."[5] One writer leaves no room for doubt as he clearly reveals a cherished goal of the humanist cause:

> the battleground for humankind's future must be waged and won in the public school classroom by teachers who correctly perceive their role as the proselytizers of a new faith: a religion of humanity that recognizes and respects the spark of what theologians call

divinity in every human being...Utilizing a classroom instead of a pulpit to convey humanist values in whatever subject they teach, regardless of the educational level–preschool day care or large state university."[6]

As a graduate student many years ago, I obtained copies of these writings and underscored these lines. Then when liberal professors espoused their views on separating church and state and keeping religion out of the classroom, I would raise my hand and read these quotations. It goes without saying that I was not a popular student in these classes.

As is always the case in the endeavors of man, there was much disagreement in the liberal community about various aspects of *Manifesto II*. Consequently, only a few ardent proponents agreed to sign the document when it was first released. To solve this problem, the *Manifesto* has since been widely circulated with a caveat making it clear that it is not necessary to agree with every detail of the document in order to be a signatory. This disclaimer had the intended effect and the document eventually garnered more signatures.

Humanist Manifesto III

The latest version of the *Manifesto—Humanist Manifesto III—*is titled, *"Humanism and Its Aspirations"*. It was published by the American Humanist Association in 2003. This version of the *Manifesto* is purposefully shorter than its predecessors. It presents six broad beliefs that encompass the humanist philosophy as professed by the American Humanist Association, but that leave plenty of room for interpretation, this latter characteristic being necessary to avoid much of the disagreement within humanist circles that surrounded the two earlier versions of the *Manifesto*. These six broad statements of belief may be summarized as follows:

- Knowledge of the world is empirically derived (by observation, experimentation, and rational analysis).

- Unguided evolutionary change has resulted in making humans integral to nature.

- Ethical values are established by humans and are based on human need that has been tested by experience.

- Humans are fulfilled in life by participating in the service of humane ideals.

- Humans are, by nature, social beings. Therefore, they find meaning in relationships.

- Humans maximize their individual happiness by working to benefit society.[7]

Although these six statements of belief are not as specific as those contained in the earlier versions of the *Manifesto*, they still support the same worldview. For example, the first statement—the humanist belief in empiricism—rules out God's special revelation as set forth in the Bible and reveals an astounding ignorance of the philosophical problems inherent in man-centered empiricism. The second statement is a reiteration of the humanist belief in Darwinian evolution which, of course, is the American Humanist Association's knock on creationism as well as its justification for supporting abortion.

The third statement makes clear that the Bible has no place in establishing right and wrong. Rather, what is right or wrong depends on human need. The last three statements amount to the humanist's rejection of God, the Bible, and religion. In the fourth statement, fulfillment comes from the service of humane ideals, not service to God and His Kingdom. Christians also believe in service, but they know that service to man comes from Christ's admonition to love your neighbor as yourself. In the fifth statement, human relationships are presented as ultimate, as opposed to a relationship with God. Finally, humanists believe that service to society is the highest service because, for them, man is god. Christians also believe in service to society, but as a way to serve the God who created us and to follow Christ's admonition to love our neighbors as ourselves.

Manifesto III is shorter and more to the point than its predecessors, and its six statements of belief are less specific, but its rejection of God is just as much a cornerstone as it was in the first two. The wording and length of the various versions of the *Manifesto* have changed over time, but its foundational man-as-god philosophy has not. Herein is found the unbridgeable gulf between secular humanism and Christianity. Herein also is found the source of the left's religious bigotry toward Christianity.

Secular humanists apparently believe they can peacefully co-exist with other religions—hence their accommodation on campus of Islam, Hinduism, and Buddhism, but not with Christianity. Although there is a philosophical train wreck coming farther down the track between secular humanists and Islam, the left has focused its animosity on Christianity because they understand that if Christianity is right, they are wrong. This simple fact frightens university faculties dominated by secular humanists so much that they feel compelled to belittle, attack, and even suppress the Christian world-view, wherever and whenever it rears its head on campus.

HIGHER EDUCATION'S RATIONALE
FOR MORAL RELATIVISM

Since man was their god, it was necessary for secular humanists to establish an ethical corollary to humanism that would render absolute standards of right and wrong obsolete.

> During much of early American history, moral education in colleges and universities moved from being grounded in appeals to special revelation to universal appeals to human nature, natural law, or reason. In other words, teachers and textbook writers attempted to locate moral agreement in something common to all humanity.[8]

Thus was born the concept of moral relativism. Of course, a fundamental flaw in the concept—and something its proponents have never been able to cover up or adequately explain—is that the only things common to all of humanity are its creation by God and its sinful nature, to things which secular humanists will never admit. Nevertheless, when your god is man, with all of his inherent moral frailties, moral relativism is the best you can do in the way of an ethical framework.

In order for secular humanism to prevail in American society, it is necessary for its proponents to control, or at least influence, the organizations that weave the tapestry of its moral and social conventions. This is why the left is so intent on dominating institutions of higher education. Anne Colby, writing for the *Journal of College and Character*, had this to say about the importance of colleges and universities:

> Of course, many kinds of social institutions have important roles to play in educating citizens. Religious organizations and other voluntary associations, the media, and education at the elementary and secondary levels are among the most important of these. But higher education is critical, because universities and colleges are the institutions most clearly charged with leading the development of new and deeper understanding through research and scholarship and preparing new generations by teaching not only information and skills, but their significance for creating the future, both personally and collectively. Higher education has tremendous opportunities for being a positive force in society as it reaches an ever larger segment of the population, including virtually all leaders in both government and the private sector. It is a powerful influence in shaping individual's relationships with each other and their communities, and we need to take steps to ensure its influence is constructive rather than corrosive.[9]

This statement clearly articulates what secular humanists surely know, and know well: He who controls higher education in America controls America's future. Herein is found the left's need to suppress the moral absolutes of Christianity and replace them with the ever-changing whims of moral relativism.

Values-Neutrality and Christianity in Higher Education?

One of the arguments frequently heard from moral relativists to justify suppressing biblical views on campus is that higher education should be values-neutral, a ridiculous argument made to appeal to the naïve. Those who make this argument claim that values should be addressed by the family and church rather than institutions of higher education. While Christians will certainly agree that families and churches should play the key role in establishing values in individuals, there are several problems with this argument. The most fundamental of these problems is that it represents a practical impossibility. Even if university faculties tried to be values-neutral, they could not possibly achieve such a goal. Another problem with the argument is the hypocrisy in it. Left-leaning university faculties invest much time and effort trying to undermine the values they claim should be left to the development of families and churches.

According to Colby,

> closer scrutiny makes it clear that educational institutions cannot be values neutral. For decades educators have recognized the power of the "hidden curriculum" in schools and the moral messages it carries. The hidden curriculum is the (largely unexamined) practices through which the school and its teachers operate, maintaining discipline, assigning grades and other rewards, and managing their relationships with their students and each other.[10]

She continues,

> that most of life situations are inherently ambiguous, and their moral significance is underdetermined by available facts. In order to find meaning and clarity amid this ambiguity, people develop habits of moral interpretation and intuition through which they perceive the world.[11]

Liberal professors understand that "people develop habits of moral interpretation and intuition through which they perceive the world." This is why they are so determined to supplant the Christian world-view with one that embraces moral relativism. Liberal professors that operate on the basis of the presuppositions of secular human-ism, that assign lower grades to students whose work reflects a Christian worldview, and that maintain only adversarial relationships with Christian and conservative students are being anything but values-neutral. Further, they do not want their students to be values-neutral. They want students to forget the values they brought to college and embrace those of the left.

HIGHER EDUCATION'S STRUGGLE WITH THE CONSEQUENCES OF MORAL RELATIVISM

Secular humanists, with their devotion to moral relativism, are continually sticking their heads in an intellectual vise, one jaw of which is formed by their professed beliefs and the other by the con-sequences of those beliefs. Left-leaning faculties cling tenaciously to the non-absolutes of moral relativism, while on the other hand they deplore their consequences. Those consequences include cheating, dishonesty, irresponsibility, and a lack of respect, critical thinking, and tolerance of diversity.

If morality is relative and self-determined, then cheating is wrong only if one gets caught because honesty has value only to the extent it serves one's purpose at the moment. If morality is relative, then my only responsibility is to my own personal needs at a given point in time. Further, it is apparent that students—no matter what their worldview may be—do not learn to respect each other, their profes-sors, or the teaching-learning process by watching their Christian and conservative peers being treated disrespectfully. When there is only one point of view allowed in a discussion, is it any wonder that students fail to develop critical-thinking skills? Finally, a university cannot possibly teach tolerance of diversity by being openly intol-erant of it. These are conundrums that liberal faculties inflict on themselves by advocating moral relativism while suppressing Christian and conservative views.

What Behaviors do Universities Expect of Students?

A study of 110 nationally-ranked liberal arts colleges found that they have high expectations for student behavior in spite of the chokehold moral relativism has on institutions of higher education.[12] The study found that "behavioral expectations were framed in terms of those that were expected and unacceptable. Expected behaviors described those that were anticipated and encouraged, and that would lead to academic growth, respect for diversity, and responsible citizenship."[13] Some expected behaviors that are representative of study respondents are as follows:

- At Vassar College, students are to participate in the creation of a community that values intellectual freedom, mutually-understood dignity, and civil discourse.

- High priority behaviors at Wheaton College include honesty, responsibility, and most important of all, honor and integrity.

- St. Lawrence University expects its students to conduct themselves with discretion, regard for property, and respect for others.

- Bucknell University emphasizes respect for other individuals and cultures.[14]

In addition to stating their behavioral expectations for students, study respondents also listed behaviors they consider unacceptable. The most commonly stated unacceptable behaviors were academic dishonesty and plagiarism. But others included possession, use, or sale of alcohol, controlled substances, and firearms. Harassment—on the basis of race, sex, sexual orientation, gender identity, religion, national origin, ethnicity, or disability—was also listed as an unacceptable behavior.[15]

What is truly ironic in all of this is that it proves the obvious, that moral relativism is a self-refuting concept. If moral relativism is valid, why the long lists in college catalogs of acceptable and unacceptable—meaning right and wrong—behaviors? The reason, of course, is that universities which have embraced moral relativism are now drowning in the consequences. Perhaps nothing better illustrates this problem than the issue of rampant cheating.

Rampant Cheating on Campus: A Consequence of Moral Relativism

As someone who has spent the last 35 years in higher education as a professor, department chair, division director, dean, provost, and vice-president, I can say without hesitation that the goal of too many college students is a degree, not an education. Couple this with a morally relativistic view of honesty and easy access to modern technologies and you have the perfect storm for an epidemic in the form of cheating. Term papers downloaded from the internet, tests stolen electronically using the photographic function of cell phones, and test answers text messaged to friends are just a few of the technology-enhanced approaches to cheating in college.

Writing for the *Journal of College & Character,* Amanda Weldy—a fourth-year English major at UCLA—had this to say about cheating on campus:

> It is when I engage my mind in questions of fairness, merit, and achievement—questions of the value of a degree—that I find myself thinking of a largely unaddressed problem in our universities today: academic cheating. For the past three years, I have become righteously indignant as I witnessed various methods of cheating: students ambushing the T.A. for easy answers, appealing to an overly anxious helicopter parent for help on a difficult assignment, or allowing a well-intended friend to do the work for them. I think all of these forms of cheating, and they often involve plagiarism, a threat

to the integrity of those who unwittingly commit it as
much as those who knowingly perpetrate it.[16]

Student cheating has become so endemic on university campuses
that protecting against it has become a growth industry. There are
seminars to teach faculty members how to spot cheating in their
classes, software that will detect plagiarism, test banks that allow
teachers to give every student a different set of test questions by random selection, and countless other tools to combat cheating. While
cheating is apparently good for this growing industry, it is undermining the integrity of higher education, and left-leaning institutions of higher education can do little more than treat the symptoms.
Getting to the cause would require them to re-think their allegiance
to moral relativism. Meanwhile, the teaching of moral relativism in
our nation's universities pervades society, encouraging cheating in
all areas of life.

THE CASE AGAINST MORAL RELATIVISM

To its proponents, one of the appealing aspects of moral relativism is
that it precludes the need for discussion, debate, and disagreement.
There are plenty of professors in universities who just want to be left
alone to do their research and teach their classes. The last thing they
want is the hassle of dealing with issues of right and wrong. Although
they are typically just as liberal as their more vocal colleagues, they
would rather let someone else fight the battles that are always swirl-
ing around moral and cultural issues. Moral relativism allows these
academic hermits to avoid conflict by simply adopting an attitude of
you do your thing and I will do mine toward students, colleagues, and
the world.

Perhaps the most appealing aspect of moral relativism is that it allows proponents to get away with doing whatever they want. It is the
perfect philosophical construct for people who do not wish to have
their behavior constrained or their lifestyle inhibited by the rules.
This aspect of moral relativism is why Ryan Dobson calls the concept "sin in a toga," by which he means that it is nothing more than
"selfishness and hedonism and rebellion dressed up in philosopher's

robes."[17] In his book, *Be Intolerant Because Some Things Are Just Stupid,* Dobson says:

> Moral relativism is not a philosophy you would arrive at by studying the world around you. If you put something under your microscope or do real science with your chemistry set or point your telescope at the stars, you will not arrive at the conclusion that there are no constants in the universe. The only way to come up with moral relativism is to begin with an agenda and then look for ways to make your agenda possible. Your starting point is not an observation of the universe, but an action you want to take.[18]

This is an important point because one of the foundational tenets of secular humanism is empiricism, which teaches that knowledge of the world is gained through observation, experimentation, and rational analysis, as opposed to biblical revelation. Empiricism actually refutes moral relativism.

Dobson gives several reasons why moral relativism is what he calls a "broken philosophy:"[19]

- Moral relativism is empty, meaningless, and purposeless. It can provide permission to do what should not be done or to tolerate what should not be tolerated, but it cannot provide hope. Nor can it give its proponents peace or answers to life's quandaries, problems, or mysteries.

- Moral relativism is self-refuting. The idea that there is no absolute truth—the cornerstone of moral relativism—is itself a declaration of absolute truth.

- People cling to moral relativism in the same way and for the same reason that smokers continue to smoke: they want what it does for them more than they want the benefits of quitting.[20]

Secular humanism is the religion of the left. It has its own bible: the *Humanist Manifesto*; its own ethical corollary: moral relativism; and its own god: man. This is not just a clever ruse on the part of Christians to render the anti-religion views of secular humanism null and void. The *Humanist Manifesto* makes clear that secular humanism is a religion developed specifically to replace those religions of the world that are based on supernatural revelation. The facts are clear. Secular humanists do not oppose all religion on campus, just the Christian religion. There is a name for this type of bias—religious bigotry.

NOTES

1. "Moral Relativism–Neutral Thinking?" Retrieved from http://www.moral-relativism. com on January 21, 2009.

2. "Moral Relativism–Neutral Thinking?"

3. As quoted in Ben Stein and Phil DeMuth, *Can America Survive?* (Carlsbad, CA: New Beginnings Press, 2004), 111.

4. "Moral Relativism–Neutral Thinking?," 2.

5. As quoted in *Humanist Manifesto II*, Retrieved from http://www.americanhumanist.org/ who_we_are/about_humanism/Humanist_Manifesto_II on May 9, 2009.

6. John Dunphy, "A Religion for a New Age," *The Humanist*, Jan/Feb 1983, 26.

7. *Humanism and Its Aspirations* (Washington, DC: American Humanist Association, 2003).

8. Perry L. Glanzer and Todd C. Ream, "Educating Different Types of Citizens: Identity, Tradition, Moral Education," *Journal of College & Character* (Vol. IX, No.4), April 2008, 1.

9. Anne Colby, "Whose Values Anyway?," *Journal of College & Character.* Retrieved from http://collegevalues.org/articles.cfm?a=1&id=685 on June 9, 2009.

10. Colby, "Whose Values Anyway?"

11. Colby, "Whose Values Anyway?"

12. Lee S. Duemer, Shelia Delony, Kathleen Donalson, and Amani Zaier, "Behavioral Expectations of 110 Nationally Ranked Liberal Arts Colleges," *Journal of College & Character* (Vol. X, No.2), November 2008, 4.

13. Duemer, *et al,* "Behavioral Expectations."

14. Duemer, *et al,* "Behavioral Expectations."

15. Duemer, *et al,* "Behavioral Expectations."

16. Amanda C. Weldy, "Degrees of Cheating," *Journal of College & Character* (Vol. X, No.2), November 2008, 1.

17. Ryan Dobson, *Be Intolerant Because Some Things Are Just Stupid* (Carol Stream, IL: Tyndale House, 2003), 55.

18. Dobson, *Be Intolerant,* 55-56.

19. Dobson, *Be Intolerant,* 49.

20. Dobson, *Be Intolerant,* 50-55.

Four

The Radical Left's War on God, Country, and Conservatives

*"The visible order of the universe proclaims
a supreme intelligence."*
—Jean-Jacques Rousseau

The various examples of liberal tyranny presented in this book are not just isolated cases perpetrated by rogue elements of the left who have strayed from the norm. Rather, they are small skirmishes in a much larger war being conducted against God, country, and conservatives, particularly on university campuses. Ironically, the tactics employed by the left in conducting this war violate the very principles liberals claim to believe in and live by. They also violate the principles of academic freedom—free speech, free thought, and free inquiry—which is the philosophical cornerstone of the universities.

In an article entitled "Diversity Dishonesty on College Campuses," Phyllis Schlafly writes:

> Diversity, multiculturalism, tolerance, and political correctness are the watchwords in colleges and universities today. The campus thought police have defined those words to enforce the liberal leftwing agenda. Diversity means diversity only for thoughts and practices that are politically correct. Political correctness means conformity to leftwing orthodoxy. Multiculturalism means all cultures are equal but Western Judeo-Christian civilization is the worst. Tolerance means accep-

tance of all behaviors except those that comport with the Ten Commandments.[1]

David Horowitz comments on the tactics employed by the left in conducting its war on God, country, and conservatives in an article entitled, "The Surreal World of the Progressive Left." Horowitz writes:

> It is not for nothing that George Orwell had to invent terms like "double-think" and "double-speak" to describe the universe totalitarians created. Those who have watched the left as long as I have, understand the impossible task that progressives confront in conducting their crusades. Rhetorically, they are passionate proponents of "equality" but in practice they are committed enthusiasts of a hierarchy of privilege in which the highest ranks are reserved for themselves as the guardians of righteousness, then for those they designate "victims" and "oppressed," who are thus worthy of their redemption. Rhetorically they are secularists and avatars of tolerance, but in fact they are religious fanatics who regard their opponents as sinners and miscreants and agents of civil darkness. Therefore, when they engage an opponent it is rarely to examine and refute his argument but rather to destroy the bearer of the argument and remove him from the plain of battle.[2]

The most effective weapon in the arsenal of the radical left is the American Civil Liberties Union (ACLU), an organization that has been instrumental in conducting the war on God, country, and conservatives. This is what the Alliance Defense Fund says about the ACLU and its efforts in this war:

> For more than 50 years, the ACLU and other radical activist groups have attempted to eliminate public expression of our nation's faith and heritage. They have done this through fear, intimidation, misinformation, and the filing of lawsuits (or threats of lawsuits) that

would: eliminate Christian and historic faith symbols from government documents, buildings, and monuments; ban public prayer in schools and at school functions; deny Christians the right to use public facilities that are open to other groups, and prevent Christians from expressing their faith in the workplace.[3]

These tactics succeed mainly because liberals dominate critical institutions such as education, the courts, and the media.

HOW THE RADICAL LEFT VIEWS CHRISTIANS AND CONSERVATIVES

It is difficult for those outside of the academy to understand how virulent the left's attacks on God, country, and conservatives can be, how deeply felt their animosity is. When I have discussed this subject with people from other professions, I find that they have a somewhat distorted view of life in higher education. They tend to view the academy as a place where diverse points of view are welcomed, and where bright people debate their differing views in a supportive and collegial environment. In other words, they think the scholarly environment in higher education is what it should be. When I provide examples to the contrary, they are shocked to have the myth shattered.

Consequently, in this section we provide examples of how the left views Christians and conservatives, quoting their own words to make our point. For example, Peter Singer, a bioethics professor from Princeton University said this about God: "If we don't play God, who will? There seems to me to be three possibilities: there is a God, but He doesn't care about evil and suffering; there is a God who cares, but He or She is a bit of an underachiever; or there is no God. Personally, I believe the latter."[4]

Such sentiments are not limited to faculty members at Ivy League institutions. The faculties of many of our country's state institutions are now dominated by leftist professors who share Singer's views. Professor Steven Weinberg of the University of Texas had this to say about religion: "I think in many respects religion is a dream—a beautiful dream often...But it's a dream from which I think it's about time we awoke.

Just as a child learns about the tooth fairy and is incited by that to leave a tooth under the pillow—and you are glad the child believes in the tooth fairy. But eventually you want the child to grow up."[5]

Writing about Christians, John Indo suggested that they be required to take a class in logic, but then opined that it would probably do no good because:

> then we would face another problem in making them respond to it. Logical thinking is antithetical to [Christians]—except, of course, when it is used to propound their strictly *ad hoc* arguments...Their limited little minds function only in support of parochialist stupidity...we must stop them at all costs.[6]

Indo summarizes accurately and concisely the agenda of the radical left. It is not sufficient to just ridicule, persecute, and intimidate Christians and conservatives—they must be stopped. As should be clear from these few quotes, the radical left is making war on God, country, and conservatives, and they intend to win.

THE RADICAL LEFT'S ATTACKS ON CAMPUS FREEDOMS

The literature is replete with examples of attacks on campus freedoms by soldiers of the radical left. To get a feel for how widespread and frequent these attacks are, consider the following representative cases:

- The State University of New York at Buffalo (SUNY Buffalo) established a speech code that on the surface appeared to do little more than encourage good manners, but the code is a wolf in sheep's clothing. The code made any speech in residence halls that is not courteous, polite, or mannerly impermissible. While universities may certainly establish codes of conduct to protect students' ability to sleep and study in dormitories, restricting all speech in a dormitory to that which is courteous, polite, and mannerly is just one more way of silencing the views of students and their ability to voice them. With such a speech code in place, any student who happens to voice disagreement with another student's life style, behavior, or personal choices could be charged and disciplined. Since Christian students are going to see plenty of behavior in university dormitories that they disagree with, they are likely to be the most frequent targets of speech code violations.

- A student-employee at Indiana University was charged with racial harassment for doing nothing more than reading the book, *Notre Dame vs. the Klan: How the Fighting Irish Defeated the Ku Klux Klan,* during breaks. The absurdity of the charge can be seen in the title of the book. The book chronicles events in which Notre Dame stood up to the Klan.

- A Christian was arrested and charged with trespassing after sharing his faith on the campus of Schenectady County Community College. Greg Davis was speaking about his faith and distributing religious tracts in a public area of the campus, when the college's assistant dean told him to stop preaching and leave the campus or be arrested, a clear violation of Davis' First Amendment rights.[7]

- Officials at Shippensburg University used provisions in the institution's speech code to strip a Christian student organization of its rights and privileges because it required members to honor a statement of faith and because it selected its leaders according to its interpretation of biblical teaching.[8]

- Two students at Georgia Institute of Technology were subjected to religious discrimination for maintaining a biblical view of homosexuality, a view that violated the university's "Safe Space" training program. The "Safe Space" program ridiculed religions that did not embrace homosexuality.[9]

- A Christian speaker at Southeastern Louisiana University was told he had to have a permit in order to share his faith. When Jeremy Sonnier tried to engage others in conversation about their faith at a location on campus designated for outside speakers, campus police intervened and informed him that he needed a permit. University officials then informed Sonnier that his application for a permit had to be filed seven days in advance. If approved, he would be restricted to a two-hour block of time every seven days. In order to apply, he would be required to pay a fee, divulge his Social Security number, and submit information about the content of his speech.[10]

- The University of Florida refused to recognize a Christian fraternity, Beta Epsilon Chi, because it admitted only Christian men. However, the university fails to apply the same standard to other campus organizations, permitting other groups to limit their membership to those who share their views.[11]

- Temple University censored the religious and conservative views of Christian DeJohn—a student and member of the Pennsylvania National Guard—saying they violated the school's speech code. He was prohibited from making religious and conservative statements in class and in conversations with other students.[12]

- The University of Maryland-Baltimore County inhibited a pro-life group's efforts to share its message on campus. A student reserved space for the Rock of Life Club's "Genocide Awareness Project" and permission was granted. Originally approved for display in front of the University Center, permission was quickly rescinded by university officials, who required the club to move the display to a succession of different locations, each more isolated than the previous location. The final location was a vacant lot removed from student traffic.[13]

These examples are representative of what is taking place on college and university campuses nationwide. The radical left is persistent and increasingly aggressive in its attempts to silence Christian and conservative speech, thought, and inquiry. On the other hand, Christians and conservatives are fighting back using the strategies and tactics explained in Part Two of this book. For example, most of the cases cited above were successfully resolved through legal action by the Alliance Defense Fund (see Chapter 5).

THE RADICAL LEFT'S ATTACKS ON THE MILITARY

One of the favorite targets of the radical left is America's armed forces. Attacking the military has long been a staple of the radical left. Following the tragedy of the 9/11 terrorist attacks on the World Trade Center and the Pentagon, our country underwent what appeared to be a transformation. Liberals, conservatives, and moderates pulled together in a show of patriotism. "We Will Never Forget" bumper stickers could be seen displayed on the automobiles of people from both ends of the political spectrum. American flags were proudly displayed and the military was once again afforded a level of respect it had not enjoyed since the end of World War II. Unfortunately, but not surprisingly, the national unity that resulted from the terrorist attacks of 9/11 did not last long. Many who claimed they would "never forget," forgot.

Following the 9/11 attacks, the radical left kept a low profile for a while, perhaps fearing a pro-America backlash, or as is more likely the case, simply biding its time. Then in March of 2003, one of its foot soldiers—Nicholas DeGenova—broke the silence. DeGenova, a professor of anthropology and Latino studies at Columbia University, said during a teach-in that he hoped the United States military would suffer a "million Mogadishus."[14] In an attempt to defend his anti-military remark, DeGenova wrote:

> In my brief presentation, I outlined a long history of
> U.S. invasions, wars of conquest, military occupations,
> and colonization in order to establish that imperialism
> and white supremacy have been constitutive of U.S. na-

tion-state formation and U.S. nationalism. In that context, I stressed the necessity of repudiating all forms of U.S. patriotism ... I emphasized that U.S. troops are indeed confronted with a choice—to perpetuate this war against the Iraqi people or to refuse to fight and contribute toward the defeat of the U.S. war machine.[15]

DeGenova dug a hole for himself during the teach-in and just made matters worse with this explanation.

Campus Attacks on Military Recruiters

Among the left's newest targets are military recruiters. Each branch of the military has a long history of visiting college and university campuses, setting up recruiting booths, and talking with students who might be interested in joining the military. Unfortunately, recruiters on left-wing campuses are easy targets for the obnoxious and even violent tactics of the radical left. What follows are several examples of campus attacks on military recruiters led by the Campus Antiwar Network (CAN), a group affiliated with an organization called the Socialist Worker.

- "Members of the Campus Antiwar Network (CAN) at the Rochester Institute of Technology (RIT) are celebrating a significant victory after the director for Campus Life issued the order to stop allowing military recruiters in the Student Alumni Union...They may have been banned from the busiest place on campus, but they will find an alternative location to recruit. CAN has no problem with changing accommodations. We'll keep fighting."[16] Obviously, the radical left relishes its attacks on the military. Members of CAN created so much turmoil on the RIT campus that the institution's administration required recruiters to move to a remote location to avoid a riot. Notice it was the recruiters and not the perpetrators of the turmoil who were acted against by the university's administration. As can be seen from this example, the radical left is aggressively pursuing an anti-military agenda and university administrators are aiding and abetting their actions.

- San Francisco State University held a career fair on September 25, 2008. Among the participants were recruiters from the Marine Corps, Department of Homeland Security, and U.S. Border Patrol. In a direct attack on the military, student protesters marched on the recruiting booths shouting, "What are they recruiting for? Murder, rape, torture, and war." The protesters attempted to conduct a sit-in at the recruiting booths. When their attempts were foiled by police officers, they staged a rally outside the building. Eventually some of the protesters were able to gain admission to the building, at which point they harassed the Marine recruiters.[17]

- Anti-military students at Seattle Community College decided to shut down efforts by the military to recruit on campus in November 2008. Here is how Jorge Torres described the situation on the website of the Socialist Worker: "When activists in the Anti-War Collective and the International Socialist Organization heard two days ahead of time that Air Force, Army, and Coast Guard recruiters had all reserved tables in the school atrium for two hours during the busiest time of the day, they quickly publicized a protest by text messaging and passing out flyers. Some 20 students—and some who were passing by—joined the action throughout the two hours. Students held picket signs, passed out fact sheets about the military and the lies recruiters tell, and chanted 'Recruiters off campus!'"[18]

Many Americans who grew up in the 9/11 era are appalled to see the military treated so disgracefully on college and university campuses. However, having served in the Marine Corps during the Vietnam War and experienced first hand some of the most violent of the anti-war, anti-military protests of that era, I know this is just the latest chapter in the radical left's on-going war against the military. It did not stop after Vietnam. Rather, it simply went into temporary hibernation. But the hibernation is over and the left is back to attacking one of its favorite targets—the United States military.

While serving in the Marine Corps, I experienced firsthand how deeply the anti-military animosity of liberal college professors can be. It was near the end of my tour of duty in the Marine Corps and I was stationed at Camp Pendleton, California. When off duty, I took night classes at an extension center of a major university. During this particular semester I was taking a biology class. Because of the crunch to make it to class on time, I often arrived in uniform. Wearing civilian clothes would not have mattered anyway. With my high-and-tight Marine Corps haircut, I would never have been confused for one of my long-haired, tie-dyed classmates. Needless to say, my Marine Corps demeanor did not endear me to the anti-war flower children in my class.

I had been warned by other Marines who lived off-base to expect the worst, and I did, in fact, experience some of what they warned me about. I was shunned by my classmates—none of the other students wanted to be partnered with me in the lab, talk with me during breaks, share class notes, or make me a part of study groups. There were also the usual anti-military comments made behind my back, but in reality, I experienced very little in the way of overt harassment from my classmates. More than anything, I appeared to be a curiosity to them, something akin to an animal that had escaped from the zoo.

The professor who taught the biology course was a different story. He took every opportunity to make snide comments about the military in general and me in particular. In fact, he spent more time haranguing the military, venting his spleen about the Vietnam War, and encouraging the class to participate in various sit-ins, teach-ins, and protests than he did lecturing about biology. The only way to earn extra credit in this professor's class was to join him in some type of anti-military protest. Completely focused on finishing my college degree, I was willing to put up with his tirades in order to get through the course and have the required science credits on my transcript. Consequently, I typically ignored him. However, one night he went too far.

We were given fetal pigs—two students to a pig—to dissect as a laboratory assignment. My lab partner was a pale, thin young man with long greasy hair who reeked of marijuana. This poor kid was so nervous being near me that when I picked up the dissecting scalpel he actually jumped back and cringed. He was none too happy about having to cut up the pig either. Unsure about how to proceed, he asked the professor for help. The professor responded by saying, "Ask your lab partner. After all, fetal pigs are babies, and Marines know all about cutting up little babies."

With great effort, I remained calm but the look on my face must have said, "This time you've gone too far." When I raised my hand to get his attention, he was clearly uncomfortable acknowledging it, and at first just ignored me. But I persisted. When he saw that I was not going to be put off and finally acknowledged my hand, I said, "I would like to speak with you in private please, right now." A hush fell over the class and the professor grew suddenly pale. I noticed that his hands were shaking. Instead of inviting me into his office for a private conversation, the professor dismissed the class claiming he felt suddenly ill.

My ride back to Camp Pendleton that night was provided by a friend who was a Navy Corpsman (medic) preparing to go to medical school. During what came to be known in the Navy as the "Zumwalt era," he was allowed to wear long hair and a beard. This, of course, allowed him to fit in much better than I could with our classmates. As we made the hour-long drive back to the base, I asked him about the incident in class and why the professor behaved so strangely when I requested a private conference. He laughed sardonically and said, "It's simple. The man is scared to death of you. These liberals really believe all of the nonsense they say about you Marines—baby killers and all that. Don't let your guard down though; he will find a way to hurt you. Radicals like this professor hate the military with a passion that defies all logic. It is positively Freudian."

After this incident, the anti-military comments from the professor stopped. In fact, he kept his distance and avoided me. But, just as my friend said he would, the professor found an underhanded way to cause me trouble. Knowing from our introductions on the first night of class that I would be finishing my tour in the Marine Corps and going home to Florida right after completing his course, this professor must have felt safe because he gave me an "F" for my final grade. My average for the course was 98.7 percent.

Emboldened by the distance between California and Florida, this coward no doubt decided to strike where he could hurt me most. It took more than six months, many telephone calls to the dean, and several letters from an attorney accompanied by copies of my tests and coursework before I succeeded in having the grade changed. Even then the professor relented only in changing my grade to a "C." I am sure he thought that since I was not majoring in a scientific discipline and his course was just an elective for me, I would not press the point once I finally received a passing grade. He was right. All I needed for my degree program was a biology course with a "C" or better on my transcript. I was headed for graduate school and had no more time to waste on a radical professor who hated the military so much that he would stoop to such petty abuse.

My fellow students and I learned very little about biology in this class. With all of the professor's anti-war tirades the class could just as easily have passed for a political indoctrination course. However, I did learn a valuable lesson about how deeply the radical left despises the military, how far it will go in pursuit of its anti-military agenda, and how petty it can be in its attacks on what it considers the enemy. And what was true during the Vietnam era is just as true now, perhaps even more so.

ATTACKING AMERICA BY REVISING ITS HISTORY

If you wish to undermine a country, undermine its institutions and its history. This is precisely what the radical left is doing in America, and with evident success. The left has made great strides in undermining the family, polluting the public school system, and dominating colleges and universities. But some of its most effective work has been in revising America's history. Alexander Solzhenitzyn said: "To destroy a people, you must first sever their roots."[19] Patrick Buchanan adds:

"To create a 'new people,' the agents of our cultural revolution must first create a new history; and that project is well advanced."[20]

Buchanan explains that in 1992, UCLA received a two-million-dollar grant from the National Endowment for the Humanities and the U.S. Department of Education to develop new standards for history books for grades five through twelve. UCLA completed this assignment in 1997.[21] Its standards have had the intended effect. According to Buchanan, UCLA's standards for history books for public school children have resulted in the following:

- No mention in history books of such American luminaries as Samuel Adams, Paul Revere, Thomas Edison, Alexander Graham Bell, or the Wright Brothers.

- The founding dates of the Sierra Club and the National Organization for Women are given special significance.

- Instructions for teachers concerning how to teach the unit which covers the traitor Alger Hiss and the spies Ethel and Julius Rosenberg encourages leeway to teach the unit either way. In other words, teachers are given the option to teach the unit as if Hiss was not a traitor and the Rosenbergs were innocent. (The Rosenbergs gave America's atom-bomb secrets to Joseph Stalin).

- The Constitutional Convention is not even mentioned.

- George Washington's presidency is not mentioned, nor is his famous Farewell Address. Rather than learn about the two terms of our country's first president, students are encouraged to develop an imaginary dialogue between an Indian Leader and General Washington at the end of the Revolutionary War.

- The Soviet Union is commended for its great strides in space exploration, but America's moon landing is not mentioned.

- Only one U.S. Congressman is mentioned—Tip O'Neill— and he is quoted calling President Reagan a "cheerleader for selfishness."

- Teachers are urged to have students conduct a mock trial for John D. Rockefeller of Standard Oil.

- Students are encouraged to study the skills and architecture of the Aztecs, but there is no mention of their practice of human sacrifice.[22]

The new history standards developed by UCLA have had far-reaching effects. Look at any history book written for public school students in the K-12 system and you will be appalled at what is included and what is not. There are now history books that give more coverage to Madonna than to George Washington. Further, America is often portrayed as a villainous nation bent on world dominance, imperialism, the perpetuation of slavery, and a variety of other evils. What you are not likely to find is any positive coverage concerning a Constitution that guarantees the rights of the left to attack and undermine America, and which protects them while they do their best to destroy this country.

HOW THE LEFT SINGLES OUT CHRISTIANS IN HIGHER EDUCATION

When the radical left is allowed to undermine America's families, public schools, universities, military, and history, we all suffer, at least indirectly. But there are Christians and conservatives, especially in higher education, who suffer directly for their beliefs. This section chronicles the trials and tribulations of a representative few eminently qualified professors who, because of their religious and scientific beliefs, have been attacked by the radical left.

Professor Emeritus Richard H. Bube of Stanford University

Dr. Bube led a seminar entitled *Issues in Science and Religion* for more than 25 years at Stanford University. It was well-received by students.

However, when Stanford's administration became concerned that Bube held Christian views and was making them known to students, the popular seminar was cancelled without notice or explanation. Fortunately for Stanford's students, Bube is not a man easily put off. Further, the left's favorite tactic of claiming that those who espouse a Christian worldview are not real scientists could not be easily applied to Dr. Bube.

Bube holds a Bachelor of Science Degree in physics from Brown University and a Ph.D. in physics from Princeton. He served as a member of the research staff at the RCA David Sarnoff Research Laboratories at Princeton from 1948 to 1962. He also served as section head for the photo-electronic materials group. He joined the faculty at Stanford in 1962 and became chairman of the Department of Materials Science. In 1992, Bube became emeritus professor of materials science at Stanford in recognition of his 44 years of distinguished service in the field. An internationally-known scientist, Bube is also a widely-recognized expert on the intersections between science and religion. He is a prodigious writer on both science and the interaction of science and religion.[23]

The popularity of Bube's seminar coupled with his status in the scientific community presented Stanford's dominant anti-Christian elite with a difficult problem: how to silence Bube's Christian views without creating a backlash from students, scientists, and Christians. What they did not anticipate—and should have—were the intellect and determination of Dr. Bube. Intellectually speaking, the contest was one of gnats pestering a giant.

Stanford formed a committee to handle the situation. Unable to provide the real reason for cancelling the seminar, the committee attempted to engage in scholarly subterfuge, throwing up a smokescreen of doublespeak about the seminar and trying to use a favorite academic tactic: paralysis by analysis. Bube was not taken in, nor was he deterred, by the committee's stalling and duplicity. He calmly answered all of their concerns, challenged their unfounded accusations, and refuted their false claims. When doublespeak and paralysis by analysis did not work, the committee upped the ante and switched to intimidation and harassment.[24]

What the committee wanted was for Bube to agree to teach the seminar from an orthodox Darwinian point of view. Like most members of the radical left, they harbored a deep fear that even a moderately friendly treatment of theistic evolution or intelligent design—not to mention creationism—by a distinguished scholar and scientist such a Dr. Bube might change the thinking of those they worked so hard to indoctrinate. It took patience, persistence, and a towering intellect, but eventually Bube was able to pin down the committee concerning their real agenda. Consequently, after two years of academic jousting with the committee, Bube was once again allowed to teach his seminar—a better result than most Christian professors enjoy.

Professor Emeritus Dean Kenyon
of San Francisco State University

Dr. Kenyon had been a committed evolutionist for most of his career and as such had won the respect of his colleagues in the scientific community. However, through research into the ability of chemicals to become naturally arranged into complex information-bearing molecules, Kenyon began to doubt the Darwinian explanation. Finally, after much research and study he concluded that his Darwinian views were flawed and that he could no longer accept them. In 1977, Dr. Kenyon began to discuss the evidence against Darwinian evolution in his classes at San Francisco State. Here is how Kenyon describes the reactions of his colleagues:

> My faculty colleagues reacted with shock, dismay, disbelief. Several faculty meetings were held and I was asked to explain myself. I was thoroughly quizzed about my beliefs about how life got here.... I don't think I will ever forget the look of shock on the faces of many of my colleagues when I explained my views. The first response was an effort to cap the amount of time students in the evolution class would be exposed to arguments against the standard view—the amount of time I would be allowed to discuss nega-

tive evidence. The amount was fixed at five percent of the course. The next move was to have me reassigned out of the evolutionary course. I have not taught it since 1981.[25]

Kenyon's department chair gave him a direct order not to discuss creationism in his class. It is interesting to note how those liberals who are so opposed to the military can be so quick to adopt the military approach of giving direct orders when there is a threat to their Darwinian orthodoxy. Then he made it clear that only non-theistic evolution could be taught at San Francisco State University. Finally, Kenyon was removed from the classroom and assigned primarily to teaching and monitoring labs, an assignment typically given to graduate assistants.[26]

To get a feel for just how vicious a tactic this was, compare and contrast Kenyon's credentials with those of the graduate students who essentially became his new colleagues as lab instructors. Graduate students are just that—students. They are working toward either a Masters or Doctorate degree; a goal they may or may not achieve. Kenyon, on the other hand, is a highly-qualified, well-respected scientist with numerous publication credits. He holds a Bachelors degree in physics from the University of Chicago and a Ph.D. in physics from Stanford. He has been a National Science Foundation Postdoctoral Fellow at the University of California at Berkeley, a visiting scholar at Oxford University, and a Postdoctoral fellow at the National Aeronautics and Space Administration (NASA) Ames Research Center. Kenyon is the co-author of one of the two best-selling advanced-level books on the subject of chemical evolution.[27]

To reduce a scholar of Kenyon's reputation, stature, and credentials to teaching lab classes is a travesty and a waste, and all because he had the audacity to question the validity of Darwinian evolution. For baseball fans, this sad case would be akin to reducing Hank Aaron to batboy for the Atlanta Braves during his prime. For football fans it is like demoting Dan Marino to ball boy for the Miami Dolphins during his peak years.

Professor Guillermo Gonzalez
of Iowa State University

One of the most telling cases in the radical left's persecution of those who fail to toe the line of Darwinian orthodoxy is that of Professor Guillermo Gonzalez of Iowa State University (ISU). Gonzalez was born in Cuba, but his family fled to the United States in 1967, where he went on to earn a Ph.D. in Astronomy from the University of Washington in 1993. An accomplished scientist, Dr. Gonzalez has published almost 70 peer-reviewed scientific papers and is the co-author of a major college-level textbook on astronomy. His research led to the discovery of two new planets and his work has been featured in *Science, Nature,* and *Scientific American.*[28]

In 2004, Dr. Gonzalez co-authored a book entitled, *The Privileged Planet: How Our Place in the Cosmos is Designed for Discovery.* This book presents empirical evidence in support of intelligent design. It was shortly after the publication of this book that Gonzalez's problems began. According to the Discovery Institute:

> After the release of *Privileged Planet,* ISU religious studies professor Hector Avalos—faculty advisor to the campus Atheist and Agnostic Society—began publicly campaigning against Dr. Gonzalez and his work. Although Dr. Gonzalez had never introduced intelligent design into his classes, Avalos helped spearhead a faculty petition urging "all faculty" at ISU to "uphold the integrity of our university" by 'reject(ing) efforts to portray Intelligent Design as science." Avalos later conceded to a local newspaper that Gonzalez was the key motive for the petition. The logical conclusion of this campaign against Dr. Gonzalez came in the spring of 2007 when ISU President Gregory Geoffroy denied Dr. Gonzalez's application for tenure.[29]

Denial of tenure is the academic equivalent of the death sentence. Once tenure is permanently denied, the faculty member in question is typically terminated.

The tenure process at ISU appears to have been not just controlled but manipulated by a group of Gonzalez's colleagues determined to silence his views on intelligent design. According to ISU's Department of Physics and Astronomy, in order to earn a promotion from assistant professor to associate professor (gain tenure), a faculty member must possess: "Excellence sufficient to lead to a national or international reputation is required and would ordinarily be shown by the publication of approximately fifteen papers of good quality in refereed journals."[30] Since Dr. Gonzalez had published 68 refereed scientific papers at the time of his tenure hearing, he should have easily made the grade. In fact, his record of scholarly publications was better than all but one of the members of his tenure committee.

After reviewing the case, The Discovery Institute claimed that "Documents show Gonzalez was denied fair tenure process by hostile colleagues who plotted behind his back, suppressed evidence, and then misled the public."[31] The Institute provides the following information, which it learned by examining documents relating to the Gonzalez tenure process and decision obtained under the Iowa Open Records Act:

- Dr. Gonzalez was subjected to a covert campaign of innuendo, ridicule, and vilification by members of his department who wanted to silence his views on intelligent design.

- Dr. Gonzalez's work on intelligent design was repeatedly attacked during the meetings in which his tenure was considered.

- Dr. Gonzalez's colleagues plotted to suppress evidence that could be used against them in court to provide proof of a hostile work environment.

- Dr. Gonzalez's department chair misled the public after the fact by trying to blame the denial of tenure on factors other than intelligent design.

- The majority of outside scientific advisors asked to consider Dr. Gonzalez's qualifications for the award of tenure recommended it, but his departmental colleagues ignored their recommendations.[32]

The Discovery Institute summarizes this case as follows:

> The bottom line according to these documents is that Dr. Gonzalez's rights to academic freedom, free speech, and a fair tenure process were trampled on by colleagues who were driven more by ideological zeal than by an impartial evaluation of Gonzalez's accomplishments as a scientist.[33]

WHY THE LEFT IS SO MILITANT IN ITS WAR AGAINST GOD, COUNTRY, AND CONSERVATIVES

The militancy of the left in conducting its culture war against God, country, and conservatives is a by-product of its religious philosophy—secular humanism. Secular humanism, as practiced by the radical left, holds that man is naturally good, or at least neutral, rather than fallen in sin. If man is naturally good or even neutral, he is a product of his environment and can, therefore, be perfected by perfecting his environment. In order to perfect man's environment—as if that could ever be achieved—it is necessary to know which environmental influences are good and which are bad.

Members of the radical left think they know which environmental influences are good and which are bad, and they do not need the Bible to tell them. Hence, they attempt to bring good environmental influences to bear on individuals and society while eliminating the bad. This does not sound so bad until you consider that it requires: 1) man to decide what is good and bad, and 2) those *in the know*— liberal elites—to have total control over all that influences society. This means they must control government, the public schools, and, of course, higher education. In fact, the educational system is the key to the whole enterprise because an educated person—as opposed to one who is indoctrinated—knows how to combat ignorance, false beliefs, and forced attitudes. Such individuals are anathema to the left.

If they can control education at all levels, leftists can control the minds, beliefs, and attitudes of educated people. With this accomplished, perpetuating leftist thinking while silencing the views of those who oppose liberal orthodoxy is a much simpler task. Dissenting voices in education threaten the left's monopoly and all of the things that can be achieved by the left for the left. This is why the left is so militant in carrying out its war against God, country, and conservatives.

This chapter has attempted to show that the attacks of the radical left on Christians and conservatives are not isolated incidents, but rather are part of a larger war on God, country, and conservatism being waged on university campuses nationwide. The liberal professors who dominate the faculties of many of this country's flagship universities feel threatened by Christian and conservative worldviews, and they are reacting by lashing out against those who hold these views, students and professors alike. Further, in attacking Christians and conservatives, the left has no reservations about violating the very principles of academic freedom that it claims to hold dear. This war on God, country, and conservatives will be won by the radical left unless Christians and conservatives decide to fight back. How they can fight back is the subject of Part Two of this book.

NOTES

1. Phyllis Schlafly, "Diversity Dishonesty on College Campuses," *The Phyllis Schlafly Report*, (Vol. 35, No. 9), April 2002.

2. David Horowitz "The Surreal World of the Progressive Left." Retrieved from http://www.frontpagemag.com/readArticle.aspx?ARTID=29654 on January 29, 2009.

3. Alliance Defense Fund, "Defending Religious Freedom." Retrieved from http://www.alliancedefensefund.org/issues/religiousfreedom/Default.aspx on January 20, 2009.

4. As quoted in Ben Shapiro, *Brainwashed: How Universities Indoctrinate America's Youth* (Nashville, TN: WND Books, 2004), 85.

5. Shapiro, *Brainwashed*.

6. John Indo, "Logic for Fundamentalists?," *Free Inquiry* (Vol. 2, No. 1), Winter, 1981, 3.

7. Alliance Defense Fund. Retrieved from http://www.alliancedefensefund.org/news/

pressrelease/ on January 20, 2009.

8.   Alliance Defense Fund.

9.   Alliance Defense Fund.

10. Alliance Defense Fund.

11. Alliance Defense Fund.

12. Alliance Defense Fund.

13. Alliance Defense Fund.

14. "Nicolas DeGenova Explains What He Meant When He Called for a Million Mogadi-shus." Retrieved from http://hnn.us/articles/1396.html on January 29, 2009.

15. "Nicolas DeGenova Explains…"

16. "Recruiters banned at RIT." Retrieved from http://socialistworker.org/2009/01/19/recruiters-banned-at-RIT on January 30, 2009.

17. Kristin Lubbert, "Protesting the recruiters at SFSU." Retrieved from http://socialistworker.org/2008/09/29/protesting-recruiters-at-sfsu on January 30, 2009.

18. Jorge Torres, "Seattle protest against recruiters," *Activist News.* Retrieved from http://socialistworker.org/2008/12/02/seattle-protest-against-recruiters on January 30, 2009.

19. As quoted in Patrick J. Buchanan, *The Death of the West* (New York: Thomas Dunne Books, 2002), 173.

20. Buchanan, *The Death of the West,* 173.

21. Buchanan, *The Death of the West,* 173.

22. Buchanan, *The Death of the West,* 173-174.

23. Jerry Bergman, *Slaughter of the Dissidents* (Southworth, Washington: Leafcutter Press, 2008), 158-159.

24. Bergman, *Slaughter of the Dissidents,* 161-163.

25. As quoted in Bergman, *Slaughter of the Dissidents,* 165.

26. Bergman, *Slaughter of the Dissidents,* 166.

27. Bergman, *Slaughter of the Dissidents,* 164.

28. Discovery Staff, "Dr. Guillermo Gonzalez and Academic Persecution," *Discovery Institute.* Retrieved from http://www.discovery.org/a/2939 on February 3, 2009.

29. Discovery Staff, "Dr. Guillermo Gonzalez and Academic Persecution."

30. Discovery Staff, "Dr. Guillermo Gonzalez and Academic Persecution."

31. Discovery Staff, "Intelligent Design Was the Issue After All (Updated)," *Discovery Institute.* Retrieved from http://www.discovery.org/a/2939 on February 3, 2009.

32. Discovery Staff, "Intelligent Design."

33. Discovery Staff, "Intelligent Design."

Part Two:
HOW YOU CAN FIGHT BACK

Five

How You Can Fight Back
as an Individual

*"Christians must be taught how
to defend the Christian faith."*
—American Vision

In his book, *Not With A Bang But A Whimper: The Politics and Culture of Decline*, Theodore Dalrymple shows conclusively why it is so important for Christians and conservatives to fight back against the rising tide of moral relativism and liberal tyranny in American culture. According to Dalrymple, rampant individualism is spreading like wildfire, including a "privatization of morality so complete that no code of conduct is generally accepted, save that you should do what you can get away with."[1] Moral relativism is the central element of secular humanism—the religion of the left—and nowhere is this religion practiced with more fervor than in America's flagship universities. This is why it is so important for Christians and conservatives, even those who have no direct connection to higher education, to join the fight to stem the tide. This chapter explains how you can fight back as an individual.

Christians and conservatives who feel discriminated against, harassed, intimidated, or otherwise persecuted in an American university have the Constitution, the law, and in most cases the university's own polices on their side. They also have the proper interpretation of academic freedom as their ally. All of this sounds good and it is, at least in theory. Unfortunately, theory and reality can be worlds apart at times, and for many Christians and conservatives—especially those pursuing a college education—the present is one of those times.

Having the Constitution, the law, academic freedom, and institutional policy on your side is no guarantee against being persecuted for your Christian and conservative views in today's left-leaning universities. As Part One of this book showed, persecution of Christians and conservatives in many of our country's flagship institutions is not just common practice, it is accepted practice. The most logical conclusion one can draw from this is that Christians and conservatives pursuing higher education in America today can have as much freedom of speech, thought, and inquiry as they are willing to fight for.

This chapter encourages you—the individual American citizen—to join in that fight. The strategies contained herein are for any individual who is concerned about what is happening in the institutions his tax dollars support, not just those who have or will have children attending those institutions. The strategies explained in this chapter can be used by individuals who care about protecting the rights of Christians and conservatives as they pursue a college education. Thinking more broadly, these strategies can be used by individuals who care about protecting our country from the effects of having college students indoctrinated and college professors persecuted when they refuse to accept the doctrines of liberal orthodoxy. Strategies explained in this chapter include:

- Supporting the organizations that protect your freedoms

- Going public with your concerns

- Getting involved in the political process

- Supporting Christian education at all levels

- Getting your church engaged

- Getting the alumni association involved

- Supporting Christian and conservative student organizations on campus

SUPPORT THE ORGANIZATIONS
THAT PROTECT YOUR FREEDOMS

If you are concerned about liberal tyranny in higher education, before doing anything else, contact the organizations profiled in this section and start supporting them. There are many organizations that support Christians, conservatives, and the right to free speech, free thought, and free inquiry. This fact is itself a testament to just how much persecution is occurring on the campuses of our major universities. Of these organizations, the ones I recommend are American Vision and Alliance Defense Fund (ADF).

These two organizations have different missions, but both missions encompass protecting the Constitutionally-guaranteed freedoms of Americans. American Vision does this through publishing, educating, and informing; and ADF through advocacy, training, funding, and litigation. Consequently, these organizations can be powerful allies for those who decide to fight back against liberal tyranny. Even if you are not being persecuted yourself, by supporting these organizations you are helping others who either are, or may be, in the future.

American Vision (www.AmericanVision.org)

American Vision is a ministry, located in Powder Springs, Georgia, that was founded in 1978. Since that time its vision, mission, and strategy have been as follows:

> *Vision:* "An America that recognizes the sovereignty of God over all of life and where Christians exercise servanthood leadership in every area of society. The future will be a 'city on a hill' drawing all nations to the Lord Jesus Christ and teaching them to subdue the earth for the advancement of His Kingdom (Matt. 5:14)."

> *Mission:* "Restoring America's biblical Foundation from Genesis to Revelation (Psalm 11:3)."

> ***Strategy:*** "Make disciples (not just converts) of all na-
> tions teaching them to obey and apply the Bible to all
> of life (Matt. 28:18-20)."[2]

How American Vision Can Help You Fight Back

The cardinal rule for those who decide to fight back against liberal
tyranny is *be prepared.* I cannot overstate how important this rule is.
What often happens in worldview clashes between Christians and the
radical left is that Christians go into battle poorly armed. Their leftist
adversaries often know the Bible and the history, values, and traditions of Christianity better than they do. This is one of the reasons
young Christians go off to college as believers only to return home as
doubters, or worse.

American Vision's contribution to winning the war against the
radical left is strengthening Christians for the fight by increasing
their knowledge and understanding of the Bible; helping them become
well-versed in Christian history, ethics, apologetics, and legacy; and
helping them solidify their Christian worldview so that they can play
a vital role in the battle for dominion. This ultimate goal—exercising
the dominion mandate—will require Christians to stand up to the
liberal tyranny taking place in universities and elsewhere in America.
In order to do this effectively and without faltering, Christians need
to know who they are in God's eyes, what is expected of them by God,
and how to take on the radical left in a spirit of Christian love.

American Vision provides books, DVDs, articles, and training pack-
ages that will help you better understand the Christian worldview, what
God expects of you, and how to fight back against the radical left without stooping to its tactics. In addition, American Vision will help you be
sufficiently prepared to negate one of the radical lefts' favorite tactics:
using the Bible as a weapon against Christians by twisting, distorting,
and quoting its words out of context.

This issue of being well-informed concerning your Christian beliefs
and their biblical foundations is critical because some members of the
radical left are skilled interrogators who know exactly what buttons to
push to confuse Christians about their beliefs. Once, during a gradu-

ate class I was taking, an illustrative exchange took place between the professor and a Christian student. The class was part of a degree in counseling and psychology that prepared students for secular counseling careers or for the pursuit of a doctorate degree in psychology.

During a discussion about counseling alcohol and drug abusers, my Christian classmate suggested that Christian counseling based on biblical principles would be more effective than the techniques we were learning. Expecting the professor—an ardent atheist with little patience for the Christian point of view—to become angry, I braced myself for the coming explosion. But it never came. Instead, the professor very calmly used the Bible to take my classmate apart piece by piece. He began by asking this student if he believed in a literal translation of the Bible. When my classmate responded that he did, the professor asked: "Then when the Bible says you should be salt and light, it means that you should become a light bulb or that you are going to wind up on someone's table in a shaker."

The interrogation, supported by distortions of God's word, went on for some time. When I or another student tried to interject on behalf of our poorly prepared Christian classmate, the professor refused to call on us. In his mind, he had his Christian victim pinned to the ground in the middle of the coliseum and did not intend to let him up. In fact, the browbeating continued unabated until—disgusted by it— several of us started packing up our books and notes to leave. Sensing that he was losing the class, the professor finally stopped.

The discussion returned to counseling alcoholics and drug abusers, but our Christian classmate was so humiliated by the experience that he dropped the course. After class, a fellow Christian and I were discussing that night's debacle. He summed up his thoughts by saying: "This is why you should never go into a gunfight with an unloaded pistol." He was right. American Vision can help ensure that this sad situation never happens to you.

Alliance Defense Fund (www.AllianceDefenseFund.org)

Alliance Defense Fund (ADF) was established in 1994 in response to the need for the legal defense of religious freedom. Think of the ADF as the Christian's answer to the ACLU. Its mission is to defend the right to hear and speak the truth. ADF partners with more than 300 ministries and organizations in carrying out this mission through strategy and coordination, training, funding, and litigation. The specifics of how ADF can help you fight back are:

- *Strategy and coordination.* When there are abuses by the radical left, it is important for all those concerned to pull together in the same direction toward the implementation of a common strategy. ADF helps coordinate and develop a common strategy when organizations wish to join forces in fighting back against liberal tyranny. This negates one of the left's favorite tactics: divide and conquer.

- *Training.* ADF provides extensive, high-level training through an accredited academy to help practicing attorneys learn how to defend and reclaim religious freedom, traditional family values, and the sanctity of human life.

- *Funding.* Fighting back against liberal tyranny takes money. ADF raises millions of dollars to support litigation aimed at restoring religious liberty and winning back the justice system.

- *Litigation support and partnership.* ADF works continually with its extensive network of partners and experienced attorneys to directly litigate carefully chosen, strategic cases that serve the purpose of protecting religious freedom, traditional family values, and the sanctity of human life.[3]

The ADF recommends eight ways that you can get involved and support its efforts: 1) through prayer in response to the specific needs posted on the ADF website every week, 2) by using the ADF's emails to stay up to date concerning specific cases and how you can get involved in them, 3) by telling others about ADF and encouraging them to get involved so the support network grows constantly, 4) by making financial contributions to ADF, 5) by ordering audio, video, and other types of presentations from ADF and sharing them with others, 6) by taking direct action with the support and assistance of ADF, 7) by ordering written materials from ADF, and 8) by arranging planned giving in the form of annuities, trusts, and bequests to support ADF's work.[4]

GO PUBLIC WITH YOUR CONCERNS ABOUT LIBERAL TYRANNY IN UNIVERSITIES

One of the most effective ways to fight back against liberal tyranny is to shine the light of public scrutiny on it. The general public is typically not aware of what takes place on university campuses. This works in favor of those who want to silence Christians and conservatives. This is why going public with your concerns is so important. The types of abuses chronicled in Part One of this book are unacceptable to the American public at large. It becomes difficult for universities to ignore these abuses when the public is aware of them.

Letters to the editor, guest editorials, calls to editors encouraging them to investigate abuses, calls to television and radio stations, and guest appearances on local talk radio programs are all ways to shine the light of public scrutiny on the unacceptable behavior of liberals on university campuses. An added benefit of going public with your concerns is that once the media takes an interest in them, it becomes much easier to get the attention and support of elected officials.

Perhaps the best example of how effective going public can be as a strategy for fighting back is found in the case of Ward Churchill, former professor of ethnic studies at the University of Colorado in Boulder. Churchill worked at the University of Colorado from 1990 to 2007 rising through the ranks to the position of chairman of his department. Throughout this time he was confrontational, provocative, and controversial. His favorite target was the United States, a nation that in his eyes could do no right. His provocative anti-American diatribes would shock most members of the public, but the public was not aware of them. For many years, Churchill flew under the radar of public scrutiny by confining his outbursts to his students and colleagues at the University of Colorado. This changed in 2005.

Churchill wrote an essay entitled *On the Justice of Roasting Chickens.* In this essay, he claimed that the people killed by terrorists in the 9/11 attacks on the World Trade Center were guilty of provoking the attacks.[5] His outrageous claims came to the attention of conservative talk radio and eventually generated so much consternation that even the mainstream media could not ignore him. Soon public scrutiny—the Achilles heel of liberal tyrants—began in earnest, and the more that Americans learned about Professor Churchill, the more outraged they became.

Americans wanted to know how the university could justify using their tax dollars to support someone like Churchill. Under intense pressure from the press, electronic media, politicians, and the public at large, officials at the University of Colorado were forced to act. They began by investigating Churchill's work at the university; an investigation that revealed instances of academic misconduct including plagiarism, fabrication, and falsification. When this misconduct was reported by the mainstream media, Americans began to question the quality of the leadership at the University of Colorado. Finally, in 2007 Churchill was fired for academic misconduct by the University of Colorado's Board of Regents.[6] If concerns about Churchill's activities had not become public, he would probably still be employed at the university using tax dollars to attack the very citizens who pay them.

GET INVOLVED IN THE POLITICAL PROCESS

If you are going to fight back against liberal tyranny in higher education, the time may come when you will need to ask elected officials the following question: "How can you justify giving my tax dollars to an institution that engages in the persecution of Christians and conservatives?" Politicians can be effective allies in the fight against liberal tyranny, but they are busy people pulled in a hundred different directions by their constituents and a variety of special-interest groups. Consequently, in order to succeed in enlisting them in your cause, it is necessary to first lay some groundwork.

Institutions of higher education, whether public or private, are political entities. This is because they depend on state and federal tax dollars for a substantial portion of their funding. Of course, state universities are more dependent on state taxes than their private counterparts, but even private universities typically receive some level of support from the states in which they are located. Further, both public and private universities depend on federal tax dollars in the form of research grants and financial aid to students. This dependence on tax dollars is what makes elected officials such potentially powerful allies.

When politicians begin to question a university's funding, it gets the attention of university administrators. Universities are political organizations. As such, they understand the importance their relations with politicians can have on their funding. Another way to get their attention is through their boards of trustees. University board members are typically appointed by the governor of their respective states. Consequently, getting involved in the political process is essential.

When politicians question a university's funding because of liberal tyranny, you will get a much better response from university officials. Further, when governors appoint university board members who oppose the persecution of Christians and conservatives, it becomes difficult for universities to ignore the abuses of the radical left. Never underestimate the power of a simple telephone call to a college president from a disgruntled elected official.

Politicians respond better to constituents they know to be *players* at the grassroots level. To be a player, it is necessary to join the party, participate in elections, and make donations to selected political candidates. The staffs of elected officials keep lists, even when they claim they don't. To have influence with an elected official, it is important that your name be on his list before you attempt to engage his assistance. This does not mean an elected official will not help you unless you have helped him get elected, but it does mean that being a player at the local level will improve your chances.

Getting Involved In State Politics: Why It Is Important

You can have the most direct effect on what takes place in public universities by getting involved in state politics. Public universities are typically state organizations or quasi-state organizations that receive a substantial amount of their funding through legislative appropriations funded by state taxes. Because of this, administrators in state universities are closely attuned to their state legislatures, and they invest substantial amounts of time and money in garnering the support of elected officials in their respective state houses and senates.

Most state universities have an individual on staff whose job amounts to lobbying, although they tend to have such titles as "legislative liaison" since using state tax dollars to lobby for more state tax dollars violates the canon of ethics in most states. Some of the larger state universities have an entire staff of legislative liaisons. State universities are deeply engaged in the political process twelve months out of the year, and they are sensitive to being at odds with members of the state legislature. This sensitivity can work in your favor, but only if—like the universities—you get involved in politics and stay involved.

Getting Involved In State Politics: How to Go About It

You cannot match the time and resources state universities invest in the political process, but do not be deterred by this fact. As an individual taxpayer and voter, you have a major advantage over a university: you are not asking for money. Elected officials know that universities court them primarily for financial purposes. They want the legislature to increase their appropriations, award special appropriations, or minimize cuts to their budgets in bad years. The fact that you are not approaching them in an attempt to put your hand in the cookie jar will be a welcome change of pace for most elected officials. However, even with this advantage you have some work to do before you can expect a legislator to take your concerns about liberal tyranny seriously.

What follows are several strategies which will help ensure that elected officials take your concerns and recommendations about the persecution of Christians and conservatives in higher education seriously:

- Approach the local head of your political party and ask what kinds of volunteer help he needs most. Start devoting some time to helping your party at the local level.

- Visit the local offices of your state representative and senator. Introduce yourself and make a point of getting to know the staff members in these offices. Often staffers can be as helpful to you as the elected official. When you need to meet with your state representative or senator, it is these staffers who will (or will not) arrange the meeting. It is critical to maintain sufficient contact with local staffers to ensure that they know you and what issues are important to you.

- Make donations to the campaign chests of your state representative and senator. This will help ensure that your name is on their call-back list when you need to talk to one or both of them.

- Get to know your state representative and senator well enough that they recognize you and remember your name. Send them an occasional email or call periodically to say thanks for taking a stand, voting a certain way, or supporting an issue that is important to you. Do not make the mistake of contacting elected officials only when you have a complaint. Constant complainers eventually get put on the "do-not-call-back" list.

- When you are concerned about persecution of Christians and conservatives at one of your state universities, take the time to develop a brief explanation of the problem and a recommended solution. Keep it brief, concise, and to the point. Avoid inflammatory language. Write it in such a way that your state representative or senator can circulate it among his colleagues to help gain support for the action you recommend.

- Ask a staffer in the local office of your state representative or senator to give you a copy of the legislature's directory for your state. All state legislatures have directories that contain brief biographies, contact information, and committee assignments for members of the state House and Senate. This directory will prove invaluable when you need to contact specific legislators who serve on committees that have a direct bearing on the issue you are concerned about.

- Regardless of the issue you are dealing with, never contact another member of the legislature without first contacting the members of your local delegation. First, this should be done as a courtesy to your delegation members. Second, it is also good strategy. When an elected official is contacted by someone outside of his district, the first thing he is likely to do is contact that person's representative or senator (or both) to determine where they stand on the issue in question. This is important for two reasons. It is bad politics to allow a member of your local delegation to be blindsided by a colleague. Second, most members of the legislature are reluctant to act on an issue unless they know that you have the support of your local delegation. Even those who will act out of a shared commitment concerning the issue in question will feel better knowing that you have informed your local delegation.

- When you are dealing with a specific instance of persecution or intimidation in a state university, the broader your legislative audience the better. Do not hesitate to email every member of your party—after first contacting your local delegation—to ask: "Are you aware that this is happening? How can we support this kind of behavior with our tax dollars?"

- Go public with your concerns. One of the best ways to get the attention of elected officials is to go public with instances of anti-Christian, anti-conservative behavior in universities. Raise the curtain and let the light of public scrutiny shine on liberal tyranny. Once your issue becomes the subject of local news stories or evening news broadcasts—both of which the staffs of elected officials monitor closely—it will be much easier to gain the support of your legislative delegation.

- Identify groups that track the behavior and spending of tax-supported organizations in your state and join the one that seems to have the most potential to help with your concerns. In most states there are various watchdog groups that watch how your tax dollars are spent. As a member of one of these watchdog groups, you will be in a good position to help identify abuses in state universities and turn the spotlight of public scrutiny on them.

Getting Involved In National Politics: Why and How?

Everything just explained about getting involved in state politics applies to national politics. However, there is a major difference. When you seek to involve a member of Congress in the fight against liberal tyranny in universities, you are dealing with a different funding arrangement. The federal government does not directly fund universities except in the case of special appropriations (often referred to as "pork" or "turkeys"). Rather, various federal agencies receive appropriations from Congress every year and they in turn make funds available for both research and practice, primarily in the form of competitive grants, but also occasionally as direct contracts. Federal grants and direct appropriations from the federal government are the lifeblood of graduate schools at major universities. Many of the research institutes established at large universities—public and private—are funded by a combination of federal grants and grants from private foundations.

Before attempting to enlist your local Congressman and members of specific Congressional committees in an effort to fight back against liberal tyranny in universities, it is important to do some research. When you contact a Congressman about abuses on campus, you want to be able to ask, "Why is Congress awarding \$_____ to fund _____ program at this university when it discriminates against Christians and conservatives?" Consequently, before contacting your Congressman with a concern, determine how much federal money the university receives overall, as well as for the specific programs in which persecution is occurring.

One of the easiest ways to determine how much federal money a university receives and how it uses that money is to download the institution's annual report from its website. Another way is to submit a *public-information request* if the institution in question is a state university. The local office of your Congressman can be helpful in determining how much a given university—state or private—receives from the federal government. Further, you can always go to the source. Federal agencies that award grants and appropriations to universities often list the amounts as well as the programs supported on their websites. Almost every federal agency awards grants to universities. Consequently, when doing research in preparation for contacting Congressmen, do not limit yourself to the Department of Education. Some of the major federal awards come from such departments as Defense, Commerce, and Labor.

SUPPORT CHRISTIAN EDUCATION AND HOMESCHOOLING

One of the best ways to arm young people for what they will face in leftwing universities is to give them a solid biblical foundation before they matriculate. This will ensure they are never bested in discussions about religion by atheists who know the Bible better than they do. Christian students in secular universities should never have to say, "I believe the Bible but I'm not sure what it says." Christians in college who are not well-versed in their own beliefs attract leftwing atheists like blood in the water attracts sharks.

Two effective options for helping young people develop a solid biblical foundation during the K-12 years are Christian education and homeschooling. As a parent you may have already decided to choose one of these options, but strategies for parents are not the subject of this chapter. Those strategies are covered in the next chapter. Since this chapter is for individuals, irrespective of their current parental status, this strategy is about supporting Christian education and homeschooling in general. There are some things you can do:

- Help raise the money to establish scholarships at local Christian schools so that more young people can afford to attend them.

- Help raise the money Christian schools need to maintain, repair, and build facilities.

- Help raise money to enable Christian schools to purchase up-to-date learning technologies and materials for their classrooms and libraries.

- Get to know the administrators at Christian schools in your community and encourage them to provide short-term classes or seminars for their senior students on how to gain the benefits of college without losing their faith. The material presented in Chapter 7 of this book will be helpful to schools interested in providing this type of training.

- Work with your church to establish a homeschool support center that includes library materials, computers, and a certified teacher to conduct the evaluations of homeschooled children required in most states.

- Use your political involvement to work for homeschool-friendly legislation at the state level as well as supportive policies at the local level.

Christian students who are poorly informed concerning the biblical basis for their beliefs become easy prey for college professors who practice the religion of secular humanism. The more knowledgeable of the Bible Christian students are when they matriculate, the less likely it is that they will return home at some point with a backpack full of doubts about their faith. Christian education or homeschooling are the best ways to ensure that public schools cannot undo what Christian parents teach their children at home and what they learn at church. Anything you do to support Christian education and homeschooling helps arm the next generation of college students to withstand the onslaught of leftwing abuse they are likely to experience while pursuing a degree.

GET YOUR CHURCH INVOLVED

If you are concerned about the persecution of Christians in higher education, one of the most difficult issues you will have to face is the complicity of churches in allowing it to happen. When Christians contemplate the reasons for the success of the left in taking over public schools, government, and higher education, the first question they should ask is: "Where were the churches?" An unavoidable fact is that the Church could and should have done more to derail the liberal juggernaut that has rampaged through American society since the end of World War II. In too many cases, the church has been a liability rather than an asset in the culture war that is raging in America.

If you find this a bitter pill to swallow and feel the need to defend your church, ask yourself the following questions before doing so:

- Does your church preach and teach the whole counsel of God or does it compromise with the secular world in an attempt to fill the pews?

- Is church discipline applied in your church or is sinful behavior ignored?

- Does your church work to develop spiritual maturity in its members or just entertain them? Does your church teach how the Bible applies to all areas of thought and life?

An affirmative answer to all three of these questions means that your church is probably an excellent training ground and support base for those who wish to fight back against liberal tyranny. If you must answer in the negative to any or all of these questions, your church—no matter how well-intended—is aiding and abetting the radical left in its war on God, country, and conservatives.

Preaching and Teaching the Whole Counsel of God or Compromising with the World?

There is a creeping secularization of the church in America as false teachers seek to compromise with the world. Churches that compromise with the world—whether intentionally or unintentionally—are supporting the left in its war on God, country, and conservatives. In his book *The Truth War*, John MacArthur says:

> The church today is quite possibly *more* susceptible to false teachers, doctrinal saboteurs, and spiritual terrorism than any other generation in church history. Biblical ignorance within the church may well be deeper and more widespread than at any other time since the Protestant Reformation.... Bible teaching, even in the best of venues today, has been deliberately dumbed-down, made as broad and shallow as possible, oversimplified, adapted to the lowest common denominator—and then tailored to appeal to people with short attention spans.[7]

MacArthur also asserts that in too many cases sermons are watered down and slanted in favor of such man-centered issues as personal relationships, successful living, self-esteem, and various how-to topics to the exclusion of biblical truth, theology, and doctrine.[8] What is especially ironic about this movement in churches to compromise with the secular world is its evident ineffectiveness. In plain words, it does not work. Those denominations and individual churches that have compromised the most, have also declined the most. Compromising with the world in an attempt to be seeker-friendly and fill the pews has proved to be not just a misguided strategy, but a dismal failure.

Theological liberalism is the ally of the radical left because it makes their war on God, country, and conservatives easier to wage.

> I am convinced that the greatest danger facing Christians today has infiltrated the church already. Countless false teachers already have prominent platforms in the evangelical movement; evangelicals themselves are loath to practice discernment or question or challenge anything taught within their movement; and many leading evangelicals have concluded no doctrine or point of theology is worth earnestly contending for.[8]

What happens in the church affects what happens on university campuses—good and bad. MacArthur makes this point when he says:

> Spiritual terrorists are plotting the destruction of the church. Scripture expressly warns us about this... Christians are not supposed to be gullible. We are not to turn a blind eye to the danger. We are not to have fellowship with the unfruitful works of darkness but rather expose them (Ephesians 5:11).[9]

If your church is allowing theological liberalism to gain a foothold, so that the preaching and teaching are being watered down and compromises are being made with the secular world, do not turn a blind eye to the danger. If this is the case, your first step in fighting back against liberal tyranny in universities is not on campus but in your church.

Church Discipline

Churches are like parents in many ways. Parents who are trying to raise their children to walk with Christ throughout their lives, advance the Kingdom of God, and be productive citizens who contribute to the betterment of society, have to be willing to apply discipline. The sinful nature of man is evident in the behavior of our children when they are left to go their own way without appropriate discipline. The same may be said of sinners in church. Consequently, churches—like parents—must be willing to apply discipline.

Jesus speaks to the issue of church discipline in Matthew 18

> "If your brother sins against you, go and tell him his fault between you and him alone. If he hears you, you have gained your brother. But if he will not hear, take with you one or two more, that 'by the mouth of two or three witnesses every word may be established.' And if he refuses to hear them, tell it to the church. But if he refuses even to hear the church, let him be to you like a heathen and a tax collector." (Mt. 18:15-17)

In an effort to be seeker-friendly and to create a welcoming, comfortable environment, many churches have eliminated the practice of church discipline. The results have been disastrous. Even the most consistent

Christian is sinful by nature. Consequently, a church that is preaching and teaching the whole counsel of God should make its members squirm in the pews a little. A sermon or Sunday school lesson that is consistent with God's Word is like a mirror; it will reveal our imperfections. What it should not do is make a sinner feel comfortable.

Churches that tolerate sin—no matter how well-intended—are not just misguided, they are playing into the hands of those who persecute Christians on university campuses and elsewhere. If your church is giving in to theological liberalism and compromising biblical truth in an attempt to be seeker-friendly, your attempts to fight back against liberal tyranny in universities must begin right there—in your church. Misguided churches that compromise with the secular world are helping to deliver the children of their congregants into the hands of liberal professors who eagerly await their arrival on campus.

Spiritual Maturity

Before enrolling at a major university, Christian students must be spiritually mature. Spiritual immaturity is one of the main reasons so many Christian students are unable to hold their own in campus confrontations with the radical left. It is also why so many give in to the moral temptations that are ever-present on a university campus. According to John MacArthur,

> Spiritual ignorance and biblical illiteracy are commonplace among professing Christians. This kind of spiritual shallowness is a direct result of shallow teaching. Solid preaching with deep substance and sound doctrine is essential for Christians to grow. But churches today often teach only the barest basics—and sometimes less than that.[10]

Churches that attempt to be seeker-friendly safe havens for sinners impede the development of spiritual maturity in their congregants. They encourage people to do what human beings need little encouragement to do: focus on themselves. Being born in sin makes us self-centered by nature, and self-centeredness is a sign of spiritual immaturity. Seeker- friendly churches that embrace theological liberalism inherently promote spiritual immaturity. This just plays into the hands of liberal university professors. A spiritually immature young person who matriculates at a left-leaning university is a lamb being led to the slaughter.

Churches promote the development of spiritual maturity by preaching and teaching the whole counsel of God, applying church discipline, and consistently seeking to follow biblical truth. Children who grow up in churches that are committed to developing spiritual maturity are more likely to not just withstand the onslaught of leftist persecution they will face in college, but effectively fight back with discernment and in a spirit of Christian love. If your church is not committed to developing spiritual maturity in its members, begin your fight against liberal tyranny on college campuses in your church.

Strategies For Churches That Do Not Compromise With The Secular World

If you are a Christian who is a member of a church that preaches and teaches the whole counsel of God, applies church discipline, and develops spiritual maturity, get your church engaged in fighting back against liberal tyranny in higher education. What follows are some strategies your church can use to get engaged in a positive way:

- Support Christian education and homeschooling in your community.

- Support Christians who teach in public schools so they can be beacons in the darkness.

- Help Christians who teach in public schools understand how the Bible applies to the subjects they teach.

- Systematically preach and teach about what God's word and law say about civil government, law, public life, economics, psychology, sociology, and the issues of the day.

- Offer Sunday school classes that prepare young people for what they will encounter in college and how they can gain a college education without losing their faith (see Chapter 7).

- Provide biblical counseling for college students to help them deal with the moral challenges and leftist attacks they are encountering.

- Support campus ministries and Christian organizations that operate on campus and encourage them to teach how the Bible applies to various academic subjects.

- Monitor what is taking place on nearby campuses and rally other churches to the defense of Christians and conservatives who experience persecution.

- Reach out to liberal professors in nearby institutions—engage them, evangelize them, and debate them.

- Support organizations that defend the freedoms of Christian college students.

The church can play a significant role in fighting back against liberal tyranny on university campuses if it has its house in order. Your church should be engaged in the fight against liberal tyranny, but remember that the fight may have to begin at home.

GET THE ALUMNI ASSOCIATION ENGAGED

One of the best places to start fighting back against liberal tyranny in universities is at your alma mater. All universities have alumni associations. The idea is to make the most of alumni loyalty, particularly in the critical areas of resource development and fund-raising. Most universities have a staff dedicated to alumni relations, often housed in the institution's foundation. Universities aggressively nurture the support of their graduates, staying in touch with them after graduation, monitoring their professional development, and recognizing those who do especially well as distinguished alumni.

A university's graduates are asked to give their own money, participate in fund-raising campaigns, support important legislation, and use their influence in a variety of other ways to benefit their alma mater. As a result, alumni-relations personnel are sensitive to the views, concerns, and criticisms of their alumni association members. This fact can work in your favor when you need to engage the alumni association in fighting back against liberal tyranny.

The first step in engaging the alumni association is to join it. When you have concerns, you will receive a much better reception from your alma mater if you are an alumni-association member. Once a member, you can increase your influence by becoming an officer. Calls from the president of a university's alumni association to the president of the university always go through. In fact, alumni-association officers typically have regular contact with their university's president and his executive staff. This level of contact and influence will serve you well should it become necessary to question the practices of liberal professors and their leftist policies. Never underestimate the influence of a university's alumni. When they take an interest in an issue or rally to a given cause, university officials listen. For example, university alumni probably have more influence in the firing of losing coaches than any other constituent group.

If you ever have occasion to go public with your concerns about the persecution of Christians and conservatives at your alma mater, do not stop with local newspapers and television and radio stations. Also share your concerns with the alumni-association members. An email informing alumni about persecution on campus can be an effective way to bring pressure to bear on university officials who are either ignoring or aiding and abetting it.

One other benefit of being active in your alumni association—especially if you become an officer—is that you will meet the leaders of other alumni associations. The relationships you establish with these alumni leaders may enable you to enlist their help in the fight against liberal tyranny. The whole point of this strategy is to put pressure on university officials from people they will listen to when Christians and conservatives are being intimidated, harassed, persecuted, or abused on campus.

The time you invest in being an active member of your alumni association may give you a competitive advantage in the fight against liberal tyranny on campus.

SUPPORT CHRISTIAN AND CONSERVATIVE STUDENT ORGANIZATIONS

Christian organizations have always been part of campus life at major universities. In addition to Christian student organizations, there are now conservative student organizations too. Christian and conservative student organizations give their members a support base for fighting back against the liberal majority in their university, a place to recharge their batteries, and a safe haven in the midst of the campus battles. One of the most effective ways to fight back against liberal tyranny is to support these organizations.

Conservative Student Organizations

In response to the increasing dominance of liberals in colleges and universities, conservative student organizations have been established to protect freedom of speech, thought, and inquiry, and to support conservative students who want to fight back against liberal tyranny. Two of the more effective of these organizations are:

- *Young America's Foundation* (www.yaf.org) This organization is dedicated to ensuring that young Americans understand and are inspired by the ideas of individual freedom, a strong national defense, free enterprise, and traditional values. The foundation is a source of assistance and information for conservative college students who attend institutions of higher education that are dominated by the radical left.

- *Students for Academic Freedom* (www.studentsforacademic-freedom.org). This organization is a clearing house and communication center for a national coalition of student organizations. SAF's goal is to end political abuse on university campuses and restore integrity to the academic mission of higher education.

Christian Student Organizations

There are numerous Christian student organizations that operate on university campuses. Some of these organizations are non-denominational, but most have a denominational affiliation. Some of the major Christian student organizations on university campuses are listed below:

- Baptist Student Union

- Campus Crusade for Christ

- Catholic Campus Ministry

- Chinese Christian Fellowship

- Fellowship of Christian Athletes

- The Navigators

- Orthodox Christian Fellowship

- Reformed University Fellowship

- University Christians

- Westminster Fellowship

By visiting the websites of these organizations, you can review their missions, sizes, methods, and services. By selecting one or more of these organizations to support financially, you can make a contribution to the fight against liberal tyranny on university campuses.

In this chapter, we have explained several strategies you can apply in fighting back against liberal tyranny. Few people will have the time to use all of these strategies, so do not feel badly if that is the case with you. An effective approach is to select one or two strategies and focus your efforts there. In making this decision, be guided by your personal interests, assets, and abilities. Choose the strategies that will allow you, as an individual, to have the most impact. Then get to work applying them.

NOTES

1. Theodore Dalrymple, *Not With a Bang But a Whimper: the Politics and Culture Decline* (Chicago: Ivan R. Dee Publishing, 2008).

2. American Vision, "The Ministry of American Vision," *2009 Catalog*, 3.

3. Alliance Defense Fund, "About ADF." Retrieved from www.alliancedefensefund.org on February 4, 2009.

4. Alliance Defense Fund, "Get Involved." Retrieved from www.alliancedefensefund.org on February 4, 2009.

5. "Ward Churchill," Retrieved from http://wardchurchill.net on May 8, 2009.

6. "Ward Churchill."

7. John MacArthur, *The Truth War* (Nashville, TN: Thomas Nelson, 2009), 165-166.

8. MacArthur, *The Truth War,* 170.

9. MacArthur, *The Truth War,* 211.

10. MacArthur, *The Truth War,* 211.

Six

How You Can Fight Back as a Parent

*"Train up a child in the way he should go,
and when he is old he will not depart from it."*
—Proverbs 22:6

In the fight against liberal tyranny in higher education, no role is more important than that of the parent. Parents are the key players in preparing their children not just to stand up to the liberal bias they may experience in college, but to rise above it and become positive agents in overcoming it. The critical concept here is *preparation.* Christians who are properly prepared, spiritually and personally, can attend any university and receive a top-notch college education without losing their faith. But those who head off to college unprepared, become easy prey for secular humanists who preach the gospel of moral relativism and are committed to an anti-Christian, anti-conservative agenda.

The bottom line for parents in preparing their children for college is this: *Make sure they are spiritually and personally mature before allowing them to pursue a college education.* This chapter contains a number of DOs and DON'Ts that will help parents ensure that their children: 1) develop the spiritual and personal maturity needed to meet the moral challenges they will face in college, and 2) are able to stand up to the biased behavior of secular humanists who dominate the faculties of major universities in this country. The parenting strategies explained in this chapter are as follows:

- Do not be a helicopter parent

- Prepare your children for life outside your home

- Assess the spiritual and personal maturity of your children before allowing them to matriculate

- Determine if college is the best option for your children

- Choose wisely the college your children will attend

- Ensure that your college student joins an appropriate local church while in college

- Encourage your college student to join appropriate Christian and conservative student organizations

- Monitor their worldview as they progress through college and act immediately if you detect creeping secularization

DO NOT BE A HELICOPTER PARENT

One of the more disturbing socio-cultural developments of the late 20th and early 21st centuries is what has come to be known as the *Me-Generation.* The Me-Generation consists of people born from the mid-1970s forward. Characteristics associated with Me-Geners include an entitlement mentality, a self-centered outlook on life, a need for instant gratification, and an aversion to criticism. Two things make the Me-Generation pertinent in the current context: 1) Young people with the characteristics associated with the Me-Generation are especially susceptible to the temptations of secular humanism and moral relativism, and 2) Young people develop the characteristics associated with the Me-Generation as a result of how they were raised.

There are several factors that have contributed to the development of the Me-Generation and its associated characteristics. These factors include the self-esteem movement in public education and the ubiquitous entertainment media that continually tells young people, "It's all about you." However, neither of these factors has been nearly as important in the growth of the Me-Generation as the phenomenon known as the *helicopter parent.*

Helicopter parents are over-indulgent fathers and mothers who hover over their children from the time they are born, giving them everything, requiring nothing of them, and "protecting" them from the trials, tribulations, and consequences of life. Helicopter parents are often people who had to work long and hard to climb up the socio-economic ladder. Now that they have achieved a measure of material success, they are determined that their children will not have to experience the same trials and tribulations they endured.

The problem with this perspective is that the trials and tribulations confronted and overcome by these parents are what made them the people they are now. Human beings develop and mature by facing and conquering adversity. It is the bad times we must navigate that strengthen us, not the good. We do not truly know who we are until we have been tested by adversity and passed the test. People grow spiritually and personally by facing adversity and overcoming it. Consequently, by "protecting" their children from the everyday exigencies of growing up, helicopter parents are inadvertently robbing them of the experiences they need in order to learn, grow, and mature. They are setting them up for even bigger problems later in life, problems the parents will not be able to fix, cover up, pay off, or make go away.

A Parenting Story: The opposite of Helicopter Parents

When I was eight years old, my favorite Christmas present was the BB gun I received from my parents. It was just what I wanted. The ribbon and wrapping paper were hardly off the box before I was outside shooting at cans, trees, and other immobile objects. My best friend also got a BB gun, and together we spent our entire Christmas vacation shooting at anything that would not get us in trouble. At least that was the case until we happened upon what my friends and I called the "old red shack."

The old red shack was a dilapidated house that had not been lived in for years and was grown over with weeds and vines. My friends and I—having no concept of ownership at that age—thought of the old red shack as "our" playhouse. Consequently, when my friend suggested that we shoot the window panes out of the shack, it sounded like a grand idea. The challenge was to see who could break the most windows in the least time. What we did not know as we happily banged away was that the real owner of the old shack lived right across the street and was observing our every shot.

About the time we blasted the last remaining window pane into tiny shards, up walked the owner with the town constable in tow. Ours was a small town; it took less than ten minutes for my parents to show up at the constable's office. I could tell we were in trouble by the looks on my parents' faces, a fact confirmed the minute they greeted the constable. My father's first words were, "Constable, whatever they have done, they will take full responsibility for it and make it right." After some back and forth between the adults, it was decided that my friend and I would spend the next several months working for the owner after school and on Saturdays. Our assignment was to mow yards, paint, trim bushes, and do various other chores as directed by the owner who, as it turned out, owned a lot of old shacks—all of which needed work.

It wasn't the work that bothered my friend and me so much, but the fact that it interfered with our budding football careers. Both of us were playing on the town's little-league football team that year and harbored childhood fantasies of careers in the NFL. Unfortunately for us, football practice was after school and games were on Saturdays. This meant that working for the man we came to think of as "Mr. Scrooge" would bring a premature end to that year's football season for us. We pleaded our case for clemency, but to no avail. The adults involved were not inclined to be lenient.

Although we did not know or appreciate it at the time, my friend and I were learning a valuable lesson about personal responsibility, a lesson that has served me well over the years. Had my father and mother been helicopter parents, they would have automatically taken my side in the dispute, written a check for the cost of the broken windows, and made excuses to the landlord such as, "Don't be so hard on them, they're just boys." I am thankful to this day that they took a different and better approach.

Christian parents are just as susceptible to becoming helicopter parents as their secular counterparts. After all, good parents want what is best for their children. Christian parents are no different in this regard. There is, of course, nothing wrong with this. The problem comes when parents fail to realize that teaching their children how to handle the everyday challenges and consequences associated with growing up is the best course for their children in the long run.

When young people are required to deal with the minor problems of childhood, they grow up better prepared to withstand the more serious problems of adulthood. On the other hand, young people who grow up sheltered from the difficulties of childhood, will be woefully unprepared to deal with the more serious challenges they are sure to face as adults. In addition, children who have never been tested by the world are not likely to fare well when they are tested by smart, determined, secular humanists in college. You can avoid falling into the helicopter-parent trap by observing the following recommendations:

- *Do not overindulge your children.* Just because you CAN give them everything they want does not mean you should. Just because other parents give something to their children or allow them to do certain things does not mean that you should follow suit. If you want to give your children something that will pay dividends for you and them in the future, give them plenty of your time and attention. Do not make the mistake of giving your children indulgence and latitude as substitutes for time and attention. When your children become college students you are going to need to monitor them continually. You will want to be the first people they talk to when professors sow the seeds of doubt and when signs of secularization begin to creep into their attitudes. Giving your children time and attention while they are growing up is the only way to establish the kind of relationship that will be needed to help them navigate the socio-cultural land mines of college.

- *Do not give too much and require too little.* One of the reasons Me-Geners feel entitled is that throughout their childhood and teenage years, their parents gave everything to them, but required nothing of them. Children who receive so much for so long without having to contribute in any way can be excused for developing an entitlement mentality. Who wouldn't? Consequently, the minute children are capable of contributing to the family in even the smallest ways, they should be required to do so. This is one of the ways they develop the personal maturity that will be so important when they become college students.

- *Do not fight your children's battles and unilaterally solve their problems.* Young people fight many little battles and go through many minor scrapes as part of growing up. They also face an assortment of childhood and teenage problems. When these things happen, parents feel a strong emotional pull to step in on their child's behalf. Parents are tempted to intercede in ways that ensure a positive result for their child, and many do. Every time this happens, the parent has denied the child an opportunity to learn, grow, and mature, not to mention solve his own problems. The better approach is to let your children know they can and should come to you to discuss how they might handle the problems they face. Parents should offer wise advice to their children, but unless the child is actually in danger they should not intercede unilaterally. As a Christian parent, you do not want the first time your child has to defend his beliefs to be in a college classroom with a left-leaning professor on an anti-God mission.

- *Do not "protect" your children from the consequences of their behavior or choices.* Helicopter parents typically take their children's side every time they are at odds with an authority figure. If their child disagrees with a teacher over a grade, the parent automatically takes the child's side. If the child runs afoul of the law, the parent automatically sides with the child. Whenever their child's behavior or choices might result in negative consequences, helicopter parents step in and do whatever may be necessary to let their child off the hook. This type of parental intervention sends a powerful message to young people—the wrong message. It robs young people of opportunities to learn personal responsibility and accountability. Many of the misdemeanor pranks perpetrated against Christians in universities— slashing their tires, painting anti-Christian graffiti on their dorm room walls, stealing and burning the newsletters of Christian student organizations—are perpetrated by young people who think they can get away with these acts of harassment because they have never been held accountable. If your children are going to learn how to fight back against liberal tyranny in a spirit of Christian love, they must first learn to be responsible and accountable for their actions.

- *Do not substitute things for time.* Some of the shortcomings of helicopter parents are the result of their buying into the myth of *quality time*. Purveyors of this myth claim that you can get by with giving your children very little time as long as it is "quality time." This, of course, is nonsense. Nobody who believes this myth ever bothered to ask the children. The truth is that your children do need quality time, and lots of it. Helicopter parents must know deep down that quality time is a myth, because they try to assuage the guilt they feel by giving their children material substitutes (toys, cell phones, computers, clothing, and cars). If the goal is to develop spiritual and personal maturity in your children, substituting things for time is a bad strategy. Helping your children mature takes time, time, and more time. Developing the type of relationship that will be necessary to help your children navigate through the dangerous waters of a college education takes time. It takes a special effort to devote the time your children need from you while balancing work, household obligations, church duties, and other responsibilities, but time spent with your children during their formative years is the best investment you will ever make.

Being a Christian does not insulate you from the deeply-felt parental desire to want the best for your children or to want to erect a life-long hedge of protection around them. But it is these parental yearnings gone awry that turn fathers and mothers into helicopter parents. There is nothing wrong with wanting the best for your children and wanting to protect them. These are normal desires of good fathers and mothers. Where parents go astray is in failing to understand that doing for their children what the children should do for themselves just cripples them.

One of the greatest gifts parents can give their children is carefully supervised opportunities to grow, learn, and mature. Of course, it is heart-wrenchingly difficult to watch the children we love experience the bumps and bruises of life, but it is like when they first learned to ride a bicycle. If they never fell down and got a few scrapes, they would never have learned. It was only by getting up, brushing themselves off, wiping away the tears, and trying again that they learned how to ride a bicycle. This is also how they develop spiritual and personal maturity.

PREPARE YOUR CHILDREN
FOR LIFE OUTSIDE OF YOUR HOME

The day our children are born they start down a path that will eventually lead them to a life on their own. As difficult as it can be to realize this when they are babies, it is an unalterable fact of life based on God's design. Consequently, preparing our children for life as adults must begin early. What follows in this section is a seven-step model Christian parents can use to help their children grow up to be spiritually and personally mature by the time they matriculate at a secular university.

Different aspects of the plan apply at different stages in your children's lives. At what point you apply a given recommendation in the model should be self-evident. However, if there is ever a question, a good rule of thumb is to start applying the various aspects of the model as soon as your children appear ready. Also, it is never too late to get started. Even if your children are already in high school, do not hesitate to apply the model. The goal is spiritual and personal maturity before matriculation. The components of the model for helping your children develop spiritual and personal maturity are as follows:

- Expectations

- Communication

- Role modeling

- Mentoring

- Teaching

- Monitoring

- Reinforcing

Write Down Your Expectations About Spiritual And Personal Maturity

With young people, you typically get what you expect. Set low expectations and more often than not your children will perform down to them. Set high expectations and your children will perform up to them. Consequently, it is important to have high expectations for your children and to write them down. What follows are some examples of expectations you can use to develop a list of your own. This is a task that should be completed by fathers and mothers working together. Both parents should agree on every item contained in the final list of expectations. We encourage parents to write their expectations down as a first step toward helping their children begin the process of developing spiritual and personal maturity:

- Learn what the Bible says God expects of His children

- Develop a biblical view of the world and life—including civil government, economics, and social ethics

- Follow the example of Christ and the words of the Bible in all situations

- Learn to think logically and to analyze arguments systematically to defend the faith

- Live according to your beliefs and do not be swayed by peer pressure

- Be a positive participant in family and church activities

- Put God, church, and family ahead of yourself

- Develop positive personal characteristics including honesty, dependability, commitment, perseverance, self-discipline, responsibility, accountability, and a sense of purpose

- Be a contributing member of your family and your church

- Learn how to take care of yourself and others

- Become a leader among your peers rather than a follower

- Always do your best in anything you undertake

- If you are ever unsure about what course of action to take in a given situation, do what will please God

Communicate Your Expectations

Once the list of spiritual and personal expectations has been developed and written down, the next step is to communicate your expectations to your children. This involves much more than just handing them the list or reading it to them. Remember, effective communication means that in addition to receiving the message, the children understand and accept it. Ensuring that your children understand and accept the message will require explanation, discussion, questions, answers, and specific examples.

For example, take the first expectation on the list in the previous section: "Learn what the Bible says God expects of His children and do what is expected." It is not enough to just read this expectation to your children. You must illustrate for them what it actually means in practical terms. If they are going to learn what the Bible says, they are going to have to commit to consistently: 1) reading the Bible individually, 2) participating in family devotionals, 3) paying attention in church, 4) participating in Sunday school classes, and 5) participating in Bible studies.

For another example, take the expectation that says: "Learn how to take care of yourself and others." Depending on the age of the children involved, this might mean such things as taking care of their own clothes (washing, drying, and ironing), making their beds, cleaning their rooms, tending to their personal hygiene, cooking, sewing, washing dishes, and doing chores. It might also mean learning how to take care of their younger siblings. What they are expected to actually do in taking care of themselves and others will vary depending on the age of the child. For this reason, we recommend that parents take each big-picture item on their list and break it down into more specific items that are age appropriate for each child in the family.

Be a Role-Model of Your Expectations

Children are perceptive, even as toddlers. They can tell what is really important by what their parents do as opposed to what they say. Telling children to do what you say, rather than what you do, is fruitless. Children will emulate what they see adults consistently do rather than what they hear them say. This means that once you have written down your spiritual and personal expectations and communicated them to your children, you must be the walking personification of those expectations.

The most powerful way to convey your expectations is to be a good role model. When children see their parents doing the things contained in the list of expectations, it closes the loop on their perceptions. They now know without a doubt that the items on the list are important. Because they have a sinful nature, children are always looking for an excuse to ignore items on your list of expectations. Do not let your poor example become their excuse.

Teach Your Expectations

Communicating your spiritual and personal expectations to your children and providing a positive example of living out those expectations through role modeling are important, but you cannot stop there. Christian parents should also teach their children how to do what is necessary to live up to their expectations. There are two approaches for teaching your children how to apply your expectations to their lives: 1) lessons that are taught on an everyday basis, and 2) lessons that are taught at specific *teachable moments.*

Earlier we listed several examples of broad expectations you might have of your children. One of these was "Follow the example of Christ and the words of the Bible in all situations." To teach this expectation on an everyday basis, you might have a nightly Bible reading, followed by a family discussion of what was read. The context for the discussion would be what Christ would do in a given situation and what He would have you do. The teaching will be enhanced if you can introduce actual situations from your lives or the lives of your children.

To teach your expectation of following the example of Christ and the words of the Bible in a *teachable moment* is an approach that can be applied in real time whenever an opportunity arises. For example, say your child finds some money on the playground and asks if he can keep it. This is a teachable moment—a perfect opportunity to teach lessons on honesty, keeping something that is not yours (stealing), and loving your neighbor as yourself, to name just a few. Parents can turn opportunities such as this into teachable moments by getting out the family Bible, sitting down with their children, showing them what the Bible says about the issue in question, and leading them in a discussion of the right thing to do.

Mentor Your Expectations

Mentoring is the process wherein a more experienced person aids in the development of others who are less experienced. In the current context, it means parents aiding in the development of their children. Mentoring is an extension of teaching and role modeling, but it is different than both of them. With teaching, you explain and discuss your expectations. With role modeling, you set an example of your expectations. With mentoring, you show your children how to carry out your expectations.

For the sake of illustration, think about teaching one of your children to drive. You will teach them the rules of the road and what the driver's handbook in your state requires. You will also make a point of being a good role model who consistently follows the rules of the road and the requirements of the driver's handbook. Both of these are important and should precede mentoring. Mentoring would involve putting one of your children behind the wheel, walking him through the process, and having him begin driving as you offer suggestions and provide other types of help.

Using the earlier example of your child finding money on the playground, mentoring him concerning your spiritual and personal expectations would involve showing him how to take the money to the proper authority (principal's office, police station, etc.). You would let him explain how and where he found the money and why he is returning it—mentoring is not doing the task for your child. Then, once the task has been completed, you would talk him through an assessment of what he did right and what he might do better the next time. Mentoring is a hands-on approach to helping your children learn.

Monitor Your Expectations

It is important to monitor your children on a daily basis to determine how well they are carrying out your expectations. Allow inappropriate behavior to go unchecked, and it will become the norm because human behavior tends to become habitual. Once this happens, changing it will be difficult. On the other hand, if you act the instant you see inappropriate behavior in your children, it can be replaced with proper behavior before a pattern sets in.

Monitoring your children and acting immediately to correct inappropriate behavior requires patience and perseverance. Frankly, some parents—already overloaded and fatigued by the other obligations in their lives—just get tired and give up. This is unfortunate because children will intentionally test their parent's resolve. If you allow inappropriate behavior to go unchecked, your children will interpret your silence as permission. Daily monitoring and correcting may be the most difficult component of our model, but it is a critical element. If it is ignored, the value of all of the other components is diminished.

Reinforce Your Expectations

As you monitor your children's behavior, it is just as important to reinforce the appropriate as it is to correct the inappropriate. When your children make good decisions, do the right thing, or show other evidence of carrying out your expectations about spiritual and personal maturity, you should provide immediate reinforcement. One of the most effective forms of reinforcement is a public pat on the back accompanied by saying, "That was good—I am proud of you."

A good rule of thumb to follow when monitoring your children's behavior is: *find them doing something right.* It is important to correct inappropriate behavior immediately, but you do not want to wear your children down with nothing but correction. Do not pander to your children, give them undeserved praise, or overdo it. Children have an inherent feel for what they deserve. Providing undeserved credit will just diminish the value of your reinforcement. But when you see them doing something right, reinforce it. Let them know that you see them doing the right thing and that you are proud of them for it. This is applying the maxim that *success breeds success* to child rearing.

ASSESS THE SPIRITUAL AND PERSONAL MATURITY OF YOUR CHILDREN

As you monitor your children on a daily basis, you are assessing by observation how well they are living up to your expectations. These on-going assessments are important, but they are not what we mean by assessment in the current context. The assessment we recommend at this point is more formal than daily monitoring and takes place when your children are approaching college age. We recommend that before allowing your children to matriculate—especially if they plan to go away to college—you conduct a comprehensive and objective assessment of their spiritual and personal maturity. The purpose of the assessment is to determine if they have developed the spiritual and personal maturity necessary to complete a college degree at a secular institution without losing their faith.

The assessment we recommend is a series of questions that parents ask themselves about their children who are nearing college age:

- Does he know the Bible well enough to withstand the scriptural distortions the radical left will use in an attempt to undermine his faith?

- In any situation, does he rely on the example of Christ as his guide in choosing a course of action?

- Is he strong enough to fend off the peer pressure to make bad choices?

- Will he be faithful in attending an appropriate church near the university?

- Will he continue to put God, church, and family ahead of self and others while in college, or is he more likely to compromise with the world?

- Has he developed the personal characteristics necessary to succeed in college without losing his faith (honesty, dependability, commitment, perseverance, self-discipline, sense of purpose, responsibility, accountability, etc.)?

- Will he make a concerted effort to remain a contributing member of our family and the church while away at college?

- Does he know how to take care of himself while on his own at college (cooking, cleaning, washing, ironing, paying bills, car maintenance, time management, joining Christian student organizations on campus, etc.)?

- Will he be a leader among his peers, or a follower?

- Will our child put forth the effort necessary to succeed in college?

- Will he seek to please God in all he does while at college?

The desired answer to each of these questions is "yes." If you can objectively answer "yes" to all of these questions, your son or daughter has developed the spiritual and personal maturity necessary to succeed at a secular university without being transformed into a doubter, or worse. If not, you and the child still have some work to do.

Conducting this assessment can put parents in a difficult situation. For example, one child may be ready to go away to college right after graduating from high school, while another may not. Consequently, parents must be willing to say "yes" to one child and "no" to another. What is at stake is much too important to risk sending an immature, unprepared child away to college. If you face the difficult decision of telling one of your children that he or she is not yet ready for college, remember what Mark 8:36 says: "For what will it profit a man if he gains the whole world, and loses his own soul?"

If you have a child who is academically prepared but not sufficiently mature to go away to college, there are other options. Such a child can continue to live at home and attend a local institution (community college, college, or university). He can also take courses online from a long list of accredited institutions. In fact, the university your child wants to attend probably offers online classes. These approaches will allow the child to continue living and maturing at home, while still making progress toward a college degree. The key is to keep your children in your home and under your direct supervision until they are mature enough to matriculate without becoming a lamb in the midst of hungry wolves.

DETERMINE IF COLLEGE IS THE BEST OPTION FOR YOUR CHILDREN

I have learned many things in the nearly 35 years I have been involved in higher education. But one thing that stands out above all else is that a lot of young people go to college who really should not. College is not the best post-high-school option for everyone. Too many young people are wasting their time, someone else's money, and the college or university's resources by going to college when they should have chosen a different option.

For my generation, college was a privilege. For today's young people, it has become a foregone conclusion. Ask young people today if they plan to go to college and they are likely to respond, "Of course I am. What else would I do?" Because their friends are going to college, they plan to go too. In fact, it is not just peer pressure that makes the college decision automatic, it is also the expectations of parents and society in general.

We have become a society in which everyone is expected to go to college and a college education is considered an entitlement. A college degree has become as much a status symbol as it has a passport to a better career. In fact, so many people now go to college that a degree no longer automatically translates into a better career. Many of the jobs in highest demand in the United States require more than a high-school diploma, but less than a college degree. For example, one of the highest demand careers in all 50 states is nursing. America has a critical shortage of qualified nurses. The educational requirement for those who wish to become registered nurses (RNs) is a two-year associate degree. Those who wish to be licensed practical nurses (LPNs) can complete their training in just one year.

Before allowing your children to pursue a baccalaureate degree, do some objective soul searching and ask yourself, "Is college the best option for my son or daughter?" The answer to this question is "yes" when your son or daughter: 1) has developed the spiritual and personal maturity necessary for success in college, 2) is intellectually capable and academically prepared for college, 3) has a definite goal that cannot be achieved without the appropriate college degree, and 4) is willing to work with you to choose a college or university on the basis of valid reasons.

The answer to the question is "no" when your son or daughter: 1) has not developed the spiritual and personal maturity necessary for success in college, 2) is either not intellectually capable or academically prepared for college, 3) has no definite goal that requires a college degree, 4) has a goal that does not require a college degree, 5) is unsure of what he or she wants to do after high school, or 6) is interested in something that has career potential but requires less than a baccalaureate degree.

Pro-College Bias in Parents: The Most Difficult Challenge

Often the most difficult challenge for parents to overcome, when trying to decide if college is the best choice for a son or daughter, is their own deeply felt pro-college bias. Some of the reasons parents push their children toward college, even when it is not the best option for them, are:

- To correct vicariously what they see as a personal deficiency in themselves. (*e.g.* "I didn't go to college, but will make up for that mistake by ensuring that my children do.")

- To protect parental egos and social standing (e.g. "I am not going to be known as the only person in the neighborhood whose son or daughter did not go to college.")

- To ensure that my children do better than I did. (*e.g.* "Because I didn't go to college, I have spent my career as the nail instead of the hammer. I do not want this to happen to my son or daughter.")

- I want my son or daughter to continue the family tradition. (*e.g.* "I went to this university, so did my father, and his father before him. Now you must continue the family tradition.")

Every young person is an individual with different aptitudes, interests, motivations, and ambitions. Some should go to college and some should not. Not going to college does not make someone less of a person. Not having a college degree does not mean they will not succeed. Look at Michael Dell of Dell computers. The most valid reason for people to go to college is that they have specific goals that require a college degree. The most valid reason for people to choose a specific college is that it can help them achieve their goals.

If you have children for whom options other than college may be appropriate, support them in selecting one of these options. If you struggle with this, be comforted in knowing that the end of the story may not yet have been written. The night classes and distance-learning programs of colleges and universities are brimming with students who, for a variety of reasons, chose not to attend college right after high school, could not attend because of circumstances, or attended before they were ready and had a bad experience. Invariably, these late starters are the most determined, committed students in their classes. Further, their maturity and experience combine to help them consistently perform at the top of their classes.

Facing the fact that college may not be the best option for one of your children—or, at least, may not be at the moment—will be difficult for some parents. I understand this and have counseled hundreds of parents facing this reality. Doing the right thing for the right reasons in this case can be difficult, but will pay off in the long run—for you and for your children.

WORK WITH YOUR CHILDREN TO CHOOSE A COLLEGE WISELY

Young people choose the college or university they want to attend for a variety of reasons, some good and some not so good. Do not allow your children to select a given institution because their friends plan to attend there, they like the football team, a girlfriend or boyfriend plans to go there, or even that family members went there. Young people who want to go to college should have a legitimate reason for doing so and an equally legitimate reason for selecting a given institution. First, a college education is much too expensive an endeavor to undertake for frivolous reasons. Second, the choice of which institution to attend is potentially one of the most important choices a young person will make. If a given institution will not help to accomplish a specific and appropriate goal, they should not consider going there.

When working with your children to choose a college or university, begin with the basics—help them clarify their reason for wanting to go to college. Once that task is completed, if they have a legitimate reason, help them convert it into a goal. Ask them, "Why do you want to go to college in the first place?" If they have a specific career aspiration that requires a college degree—physician, lawyer, engineer, architect, accountant, teacher, scientist, mathematician—getting the necessary college degree becomes their goal. With such a goal in place, it becomes less difficult to choose an appropriate college or university. However, if your children want to go to college because that is what their friends are doing, to get out from under your supervision, or because they do not know what they want to do, they are not yet ready for college.

College is an expensive and dangerous place for a young person to figure out who they are, or decide what they want to do with their lives. These kinds of issues should be sorted out before matriculating. Aimless young people make easy prey for leftist professors looking for converts. One of the things Christians will need in order to persevere in completing their college degrees in left-leaning institutions is a strong commitment to a specific goal. Commitment is a powerful motivator for sticking it out when the path to a college degree gets rocky. Commitment to a specific goal, coupled with spiritual and personal maturity, will get Christian students through the roadblocks liberal professors are likely to erect on campus.

Once your children have a legitimate reason for going to college—such as a goal that cannot be achieved without a specific college degree—they are ready to work with you in selecting a college or university. This process should be undertaken with great care. In addition to questions about the cost of tuition, books, and other expenses, the following questions should be answered before selecting where they will attend:

- *Does the institution offer the degree needed?* This question can be easily answered by visiting the institution's web site.

- *What is the institution's record concerning how it treats Christian and conservative students and professors? How has the institution responded to instances of persecution against Christian and conservative students?* The Alliance Defense Fund, Students for Academic Freedom, Foundation for Individual Rights in Education, and the Young America's Foundation all monitor these issues and can answer both of these questions.

- *What kinds of support organizations for Christians and conservatives operate on the institution's campus?* Does the institution have chapters of Christian and conservative student organizations your child can join? What are these organizations and what is their current status (*i.e.* active, supported or opposed by the institution's administration, well-funded or struggling, etc.)? The availability part of this question can be answered by reviewing the institution's most recent catalog, which is probably available online. All student organizations will be listed in the catalog. The status aspect of the question can be answered by contacting the student organizations directly.

- *Does the institution have a "speech code" that is really just a tool for suppressing free speech?* If the institution has a speech code it will be published in either its catalog or student handbook, or both. These documents are typically available online at the institution's web site.

- *How are dormitories handled? Are they co-educational or segregated by gender? Are students allowed to select a roommate or does the institution assign roommates? What recourse does a student have if assigned an incompatible roommate?* It is not uncommon for a Christian or conservative student to be assigned a college roommate who is completely incompatible (homosexual, drinker, drug user, all-night party person, etc.). These questions should be posed to the dean of students or his designee either directly or in a telephone call so that follow-up questions can be asked. Dormitory arrangements are often one of the biggest challenges Christian and conservative students face in college.

Great care should be taken in the selection of your children's colleges or universities. It has been my experience during almost 35 years in higher education that young people can be incredibly cavalier in choosing an institution to attend, and that often their parents do little better. Students tend to choose on the basis of personal attraction (*i.e.* they like the sports teams, a friend, or a girlfriend or boyfriend plans to go there, it is far away from mom and dad, etc.). Parents tend to choose on the basis of money (*e.g.* the school that will provide the best scholarship or financial aid is chosen regardless of other factors that, in the long run, are more important).

For decades, I have helped students and parents pick up the pieces and start over after choosing poorly when selecting a college or university. After going away to the wrong institution for the wrong reasons, they find themselves in my office wondering what to do. Frankly, in most of these cases, resurrecting the student's academic career is a much easier task than helping get his life back on track. For many, attending the wrong institution for the wrong reasons turned out to be a traumatic experience completely at odds with their beliefs and level of maturity. Ensuring that your children are spiritually and personally mature before matriculating and choosing their college or university wisely can prevent this type of trauma for them and you.

ENSURE THAT YOUR COLLEGE STUDENT JOINS A LOCAL CHURCH WHILE IN COLLEGE

Christian students should never try to go it alone after matriculating at a college or university, especially one that is dominated by the radical left. Pursuing a college education is difficult enough under even the best circumstances. When you add the moral challenges intrinsic to college campuses and the roadblocks that are sure to be erected by liberal professors committed to secular humanism and moral relativity, the situation becomes more difficult. Consequently, it is important for Christian students to have a support base to regularly bolster their spirits, remind them of what is real and true, and refocus them on what really matters. A key part of this support base must be the church.

Too many Christian students go away to college and never attend church until they come home on holidays to visit their parents. In many cases, the parents find that their college student is reluctant to attend church, that it is no longer a priority in his life. Do not let this happen with your children. Get them involved with an appropriate church in the community around their college or university. Further, do not let them substitute the watered-down, non-denominational, non-doctrinal chapel services that are available at some institutions, for a church that will have high expectations of them. Your children should be part of a church family that will support them during their college years, hold them accountable, and remind them of what is true and right.

ENCOURAGE YOUR COLLEGE STUDENT TO JOIN APPROPRIATE STUDENT ORGANIZATIONS

Even the most devout and mature Christian and conservative students will need a support base as they deal with the daily uphill battle against liberal bias on campus. In most colleges and universities, there are chapters of national organizations that students may join. Those that we recommend have been mentioned several times in this book. They include the Young America's Foundation, Students for Academic Freedom, and a variety of church-affiliated organizations. These organizations can mean the difference between success and failure for Christian and conservative college students.

You will be able to determine which organizations are available to your children by visiting the web sites of colleges and universities you are considering. Some institutions include a list of all student organizations in their catalog. Others post them on their web site under the heading, "Student Organizations." We recommend that you and your children make contact with an officer in the organization that interests you and find out if the organization would be helpful. Remember, organizations such as Young America's Foundation and Students for Academic Freedom focus on protecting your children's freedom of speech. Church-affiliated student organizations are more concerned with their spiritual needs. Consequently, we recommend that college students join one of each type of organization.

MONITOR YOUR COLLEGE STUDENT'S WORLDVIEW AND ACT IMMEDIATELY

During my years in higher education, I have been approached numerous times by parents who sent their children away to a secular institution, only to have liberal professors turn their worldview upside down. I have had distraught parents tell me, "We don't even recognize our son since he went away to college. He has become the type of person we warned him about." In every case I have given parents the same advice: bring your college student home right now. A college education may be important, but it is not worth losing his soul.

If you send your children away to a college or university, maintain contact with them continually through email, telephone calls, and face-to face visits. Make sure they come home for holidays rather than "hanging out with friends." Also, have them come home for the summer, live in your home, and interact with your family, as well as their church family. Use on-going contact with your college student to monitor his attitude toward your family's values and the biblical principles on which he was raised. Act immediately if you notice creeping secularization.

When young Christians and conservatives are placed in a situation that is so dominantly liberal, they can begin to adopt new attitudes, language, and perspectives without even realizing it. Soon they find themselves doubting their beliefs and questioning the values of their parents. This is why it is so important to ensure that your college student joins a good church in the university's community as well as supportive student organizations. After spending all day hearing left-leaning lectures, it is important that they have somewhere to go where they can hear the other side. After being subjected to liberal indoctrination all week, it is important for your college student to have a good church to attend on Sunday to get regrounded in the truth.

A hard reality some parents may face is the need to pull their student out of college temporarily and bring him home. Sometimes our children are not as spiritually and personally mature as we thought they were. At other times, the pressure of an environment so dominantly liberal is just more than they can withstand. Whatever the reason, if you notice creeping secularization in your college student, and it persists in spite of your efforts to deal with it, bring your son or daughter home for a refresher course in God and family. Do not let fears of your college student falling behind be an issue.

In an era in which distance-learning opportunities are so readily available, keeping up with studies while living at home should be no problem. However, let us be clear on this issue, falling behind the peer group is not as bad as losing one's faith. If your college student has to choose between staying on track in college and sacrificing his core beliefs, the choice should be obvious. Besides, the student bodies of colleges and universities are now so age-diverse that graduating with a peer group is no longer an issue. Choose almost any college or university graduation and you will find people receiving degrees who range in age from very young to very old. During my career, I have shaken the hands of college graduates ranging in age from 14 to 84 years old.

No role is more important in the fight against liberal tyranny than that of the parent. Raising your children to be spiritually and personally mature before going to college is the same as properly training and equipping a soldier before sending him into battle. Teach your children biblical truth and be a consistent example for them of living out that truth every day. Then if they go away to college, they may just change the hearts and minds of liberals, instead of having their hearts and minds changed by them.

Seven

How You Can Fight Back as a Student

"If winning isn't important, why do they keep score?"
—Adolph Rupp

The ultimate foot soldier in the fight against liberal tyranny on college and universities is you—the student. Like foot soldiers in every battle, you will bear the burden of standing eye to eye with the adversary every day and you, more than anyone else, will feel the heat of battle. Therefore, it is essential that as a Christian and conservative student you know what you are up against and be prepared. For example, consider the case of Jonathan Lopez, a California college student who was verbally abused by his professor for daring to give a pro-marriage speech in class.

The context for this case of liberal tyranny is that just a month before Lopez gave his speech, California voters had amended the state's constitution to protect traditional marriage. As part of his speech, Lopez read the dictionary definition of marriage. This was as far as he got. His professor stopped the class, called Lopez a "fascist b____d" and announced that anyone in class who was offended could leave. When the entire class chose to stay, the leftist professor preempted Lopez by dismissing the class on the spot.[1]

Unfortunately, instances of abuse such as this are common in today's left-leaning colleges and universities. This is why attaining a college degree is more difficult for Christian and conservative students than it is for non-believers. Not only will you have to satisfy the requirements of your professors and the institution, you will have to do so while defending yourself and your beliefs. Like any soldier, before engaging your adversary you need to: 1) be prepared, and 2) adopt effective strategies. Your preparation has been a life-long endeavor that should have resulted in spiritual and personal maturity, and a biblical worldview. If you would like to conduct a self-assessment concerning your spiritual and personal maturity, read the previous chapter on parenting strategies in the fight against liberal tyranny.

This chapter assumes that you have developed the spiritual and personal maturity necessary to pursue a college education without losing your faith, and recommends the following strategies for succeeding in a secular college without compromising your Christian and conservative principles:

- Know what to expect

- Be part of campus life without being compromised by it

- Use critical thinking as a tool in refuting the false and/or misguided views of the left

- Fight back, but do so in a spirit of Christian love

- Stand up to temptation

- Persevere against liberal tyranny in all of its forms

- Go on the offensive against liberal tyranny

KNOW WHAT TO EXPECT

The university campus has been described as *Disneyworld without the rides.* Just like the Magic Kingdom, the university campus bears little resemblance to the real world. It is a one-of-a-kind environment like nothing you have ever experienced or ever will again after college. Consequently, it can seem like an alien environment, especially to Christian and conservative students. If you and your parents followed our recommendations from Chapter 6, the culture shock you feel upon arriving on campus should be mitigated somewhat. But the truth is that nothing can fully prepare you for the campus environment, neither the good aspects nor the bad. The best you can do is learn as much as possible about what to expect and then quickly learn the rest after arriving on campus.

What follows are some of the emotions, feelings, and fears you are likely to experience early in your college career:

- *Homesickness.* For many new students, going away to college is the first time they have been away from their families for an extended period. Moving outside of your comfort zone—family, friends, church, and familiar surroundings—can be disconcerting for even the most eager college student. Consequently, homesickness is a common reaction for new college students. Rather than fret about it, take your homesickness as a reminder of what is most important in your life. Look at college as temporary, but your family and your relationship with God as permanent. Stay in touch with your family by telephone, email, and visits throughout your time in college and join a good church in the community near your campus so that you have a church family to lean on for support.

- *Alienation.* Christian and conservative students often feel as if they have landed on an alien planet when they first arrive on campus. For students raised in a Christian environment, a university campus can seem like a strange new world, where anything and everything goes. Much of what you will observe upon arriving on campus will be at odds with how you have been raised. As a result, you are likely to feel alienated from the crowd. Drinking, drugs, immodest dress, language, recreational sex, and various forms of immorality may seem like the norm. Whatever forms of worldly behavior are practiced in secular culture will be seen on a university campus and magnified in both frequency and intensity. The key for Christian and conservative students is to remember that you are to be in the world but not of it. In fact, if you stop feeling alienated during your college years there may be a problem.

- *Loneliness.* Christian and conservative college students often feel alone in the midst of a crowd. Although there are plenty of students on campus, they are so different in their worldviews and personal habits that it may be difficult for you to relate to them. Consequently, one of the first things you will want to do after arriving on campus is join a Christian and a conservative student organization. This will allow you to interact with other students who share your values and understand your concerns, vulnerabilities, and fears. This strategy is explained later in this chapter.

- *Besieged.* Christian and conservative students often feel as if they are under attack, besieged on all sides by professors and fellow students who disagree with their views and are openly hostile to them. If you feel this way, you are right— you are under attack. This fact is precisely why we wrote this book.

BE PART OF CAMPUS LIFE
WITHOUT BEING COMPROMISED BY IT

Christians understand the challenge of being in the world without being of it. Having to meet this challenge should not be new to you. Christians certainly do not escape this situation by going to college. In fact, college just increases the magnitude of the problem. Almost everything about the world that Christians should avoid being part of can be readily found on a university campus. The key to this strategy is learning how to interact in a positive way with non-believers while not being seduced by their views or changed by their behavior.

- *Remember at all times who you are and what you believe.* You will not be on campus long before opportunities to do things you should not do will present themselves. Opportunities to drink, use drugs, cheat on school work, engage in recreational sex, and participate in other forms of immoral behavior will abound during your college years. No matter what you see the crowd doing, remember at all times who you are and what you believe. Do not hide your Christianity to avoid offending others. Those who would lead you down the wrong path are not worthy of your concern. Further, do not underestimate the power of your positive example to influence weak students who are just going along to get along. Your refusal to participate in the wrong kinds of activities might give another person the determination to refuse. On the other hand, if a student who knows that you are a Christian sees you going along with the crowd, he might use your poor example as "permission" to go along too. Remember, you are a child of God, committed to following the example of Jesus Christ, and you know right from wrong. Be prepared during your college years to follow the advice made famous by Nancy Reagan: "Just say NO."

- *Join appropriate student organizations.* You will soon learn that even the strongest Christians and the most dedicated conservatives need a base of like-minded supporters during their college years. One of the best ways to establish a base of support after arriving on campus is to join an appropriate student organization. If you and your parents followed our advice from the previous chapter, you have already chosen one or two organizations to join. If not, you can quickly determine which organizations are available on campus by visiting the Student Activities office at your institution. To review, campus student organizations that are typically available on university campuses include the following: Young America's Foundation, Students for Academic Freedom, Baptist Collegiate Ministry, Campus Outreach, Fellowship of Christian Athletes, Intervarsity Christian Fellowship, Presbyterian Student Organization, Reformed University Fellowship, Wesley Foundation, and a variety of others supported by specific denominations. These organizations can provide a friendly environment in which to recharge your intellectual and spiritual batteries, gain respite from your daily battles with liberal activists, and interact with others who share your beliefs and challenges.

- *Be a witness for Christ.* Every Christian should be an evangelist. We are called not just to know God, but to help others know God. If you join a Christian student organization, it will probably organize campus activities in which you can participate. But you do not have to wait for organized activities sponsored by Christian organizations. By your example, you can be a witness for Christ every day. Even the most ardently atheistic college professor will notice the example of a Christian student who is always: 1) in class on time, 2) well-prepared, and 3) first to turn in required assignments. Even leftist professors who reject your views will appreciate your diligence. Further, your fellow students will notice: 1) your example of articulating your views in a calm and reasoned manner, 2) the fact that you are thoroughly prepared and know your subject well, 3) your ability to disagree without being disagreeable, 4) your steadfastness in persisting in your beliefs even when browbeaten by a left-leaning professor, and 5) your perseverance in continuing to swim upstream against the current of liberalism. This is why no matter how poorly your professors or fellow students behave, your response must always be tempered by Christian love.

CRITICAL THINKING AS A TOOL IN REFUTING THE FALSE AND/OR MISGUIDED VIEWS OF THE LEFT

The Achilles heel of secular humanists is logic. Their views are built on a foundation of sand. One of the best ways to refute the assertions of a liberal is by extending them to their logical conclusions. For example, one of the foundational planks in the platform of the left is what they call "pro-choice," by which they mean pro-abortion. The reason pro-abortion liberals insist that an unborn baby is not a human being is because of where the logic leads if they admit the obvious fact of its humanity.

If an unborn baby is a human being, rather than just a "fetus," logic makes clear that pro-abortion advocates support killing for the sake of convenience. If this is the case, can the elderly, homeless, mentally-disabled, and others among us, who at times are certainly inconvenient, be killed too. Logic would say "yes." This is just one example of why it is important for you to develop critical thinking skills. By thinking critically, you can find the holes in the arguments of liberals, point them out, and refuse to be swayed by them.

What Is Critical Thinking?

Critical thinking involves applying sound reasoning, good judgment, and objective logic when analyzing and interpreting the input of others. Critical thinking will help you recognize bias in the arguments of others, assess the motives behind the views professed by others, distinguish between facts and opinions, distinguish between explanations and rationalizations, recognize fundamental issues, distinguish between causes and symptoms, and use facts to eliminate the fog of ambiguity.[2]

Differences Between Critical Thinkers and Non-Critical Thinkers

Non-critical thinkers tend to be closed-minded, inflexible, and stubborn when discussing issues. You are probably going to experience these characteristics first-hand during your college years. For example, these traits describe the professor in the example cited at the beginning of this chapter when Jonathan Lopez was profanely interrupted and his pro-marriage speech cut short by a professor who displayed anything but critical thinking skills. Non-critical thinkers also tend to be overly confident and arrogant about their views. Once again, you will probably experience this during your college years. Non-critical thinkers often react on the basis of emotion, rather than intellectual curiosity or scholarly inquiry.[3]

Their manifest failings as critical thinkers are why some liberal professors resort to verbal abuse, intimidation, and persecution in their dealings with Christian and conservative students and colleagues. Some of the best examples of this phenomenon are found in the debates raging on university campuses about intelligent design. Opponents of intelligent design, are typically highly-educated scholars who have gained a measure of credibility among their colleagues. Since this is the case, one would expect that in debating advocates of intelligent design, they would be able to calmly and rationally explain why they disagree with the concept. Instead, the Darwinists often stoop to the kind of name-calling, mudslinging, and dirty tactics associated with old-fashioned, big-city politics. By using tactics that are so pointedly at odds with what one would expect of highly-educated scholars, the Darwinists only damage their own credibility in the long run.

Overcoming the Faulty Reasoning of Rabid Secular Humanists

As a critical thinker in a left-leaning university, you will often find yourself having to deal with the faulty reasoning of secular humanists who are so determined to advance their anti-God, anti-conservative agenda, that their scholarly logic is supplanted by visceral emotion. What follows are the most common manifestations of this phenomenon. As a critical thinker, you should prepare yourself to recognize the errors in logic of your leftwing adversaries and be prepared to point them out during discussions and debates. Feldman lists the following tactics and errors of non-critical thinkers:[4]

- *Introducing irrelevant information.* Assume that your class is discussing the issue of gun control. Your professor, arguing that the Second Amendment should be rescinded says, "The founding fathers did not anticipate the development of assault weapons like AK-47s with thirty-round magazines." As a critical thinker, you could point out the irrelevance of his argument by explaining that the relative capabilities of different weapons had nothing to do with the original deliberations about the Second Amendment. Rather, the founding fathers were determined to ensure that citizens would always have the right and the ability to defend themselves and their families. The context for the Second Amendment was the founders' fear of an armed military force being imposed on American citizens—as the British troops had been prior to the War for Independence—not the fire-power of the weapons available to Americans at any given point.

- *Oversimplifying.* Assume the discussion in your class is about the immoral practice of abortion. Your professor, who is an ardent pro-abortionist, says: "It's a woman's body we are talking about. I should be able to do what I want with my body." As a critical thinker, you could point out the oversimplification in her argument by explaining that abortion is not just something a woman does with her body, like getting a tattoo or applying makeup. Further, there is more involved than just her body, such as the life of the child and the coarsening of society that comes with such practices as abortion.

- *Arguing from ignorance.* Assume the discussion in your dormitory is about service in the military. A fellow student says, "I will never serve in the military. All they do is teach you how to kill innocent women and children." As a critical thinker, you could point out that this student is arguing from ignorance. First, he has never served in the military, so he has no basis for making such a claim. Second, if he had ever served, or if he had studied the question in even a cursory manner, he would know better.

- *Using circular reasoning.* Circular reasoning is reasoning that is supported only by itself. Assume you are discussing the concept of universal healthcare with some friends in the student union. An advocate of the concept says, "We should adopt universal healthcare right now. It is the best way to provide healthcare in a civilized society." When another student inquires as to the basis for this assertion, the universal healthcare advocate says, "I just know it is the right thing to do." You could point out that this is circular reasoning. Because it has no basis in fact, it raises many questions, but answers none.

- *Using the destructive* ad hominem *argument.* This is the favorite tactic of the radical left. It means that when you cannot refute your opponent's argument, attack your opponent or his character (bearing false witness against your neighbor). The case of the California professor who called Jonathan Lopez a "fascist b_____d" during his speech in favor of traditional marriage, is an example of the destructive *ad hominem* argument taken to an extreme—an increasingly common practice on university campuses. Had you been a student in this class, you could have pointed out that the professor's opinion of the student's parentage was irrelevant. Lopez had advocated a specific point of view in his speech, one that California voters had just shown their overwhelming support for at the ballot box. If the professor disagreed, he should have refuted the student's point of view—if he could—or, if unable to do that, offered an alternative. Attacking the student in mid-speech—using the destructive *ad hominem* argument—is beneath the dignity of a college professor.

- *Using the slippery slope argument.* The slippery slope argument suggests that taking a certain action will automatically lead to an ever worsening set of circumstances. The twisted logic behind this argument is: "Give them an inch and they will take a mile." Darwinists use this argument in their attempts to silence creationists and advocates of intelligent design. Assume that your class is discussing Darwinism versus creationism. Your professor angrily asserts, "Give Christians an inch in this battle and they will turn our universities into church schools!" As a critical thinker, you could point out that the professor is using the slippery slope argument and that giving Christians opportunities to advocate on behalf of their beliefs, without fear of persecution, is a long way from converting public universities into "church schools."

- *Using inflammatory language.* It is a sad commentary that this has become a favored tactic of the radical left in colleges and universities. Like using the *ad hominem* argument, using inflammatory language is an act of emotion fueled by desperation. When Darwinists refer to creationists as "stupid" or when advocates of homosexual marriage refer to Christians as "fascists," they are using this tactic. Assume your class is discussing the case presented earlier in this book in which Guillermo Gonzalez was denied tenure because of his views on intelligent design. Your professor continually refers to Dr. Gonzalez by using such inflammatory terms as "moron" and "idiot." As a critical thinker, you could point out that calling a fellow professor with the credentials of Dr. Gonzalez such names is inflammatory and hardly what you would expect from a college professor. If you really wanted to challenge your left-leaning professor, you might ask him how his own credentials compare with those of Dr. Gonzalez and ask what that says about his being a moron or an idiot.

- *Using intimidating language.* This has become another favored tactic of the radical left on university campuses. It works like this: If you cannot refute your opponent's views with logic, reason, or facts, use intimidation to prevent him from stating those views. Assume that your class is discussing the issue of stem cell research. A Christian student raises several questions about the ethics of it. The professor responds by saying, "Anyone in this class who holds your views is not likely to pass." As a critical thinker, you could point out that this is blatant intimidation, a practice at odds with the scholarly approach and the professed liberal idea of academic freedom.

- *Appealing to compassion.* One of the ploys of the radical left—especially when trying to convert naïve Christians who may not be as well-versed in their own beliefs as they should be—is to appeal to compassion. After all, as Christians, shouldn't we follow Christ's example of compassion? Assume your class is discussing the issue of allowing homosexual couples to adopt children. Your professor says, "How could anyone possibly object to this when the gay couple will be good parents who will provide a loving and supportive home for these poor abandoned children?" As a critical thinker, you might point out that the professor is astutely, but disingenuously, using compassion to gain the support of his listeners without providing the whole story. His argument on behalf of the "poor abandoned children" has an obvious shortcoming: it assumes that the children in question cannot be adopted by Christian or other parents who would also provide them a "loving and supportive home," without all of the confusion and socio-cultural stress inherent in a homosexual adoption.

- *Using ridicule.* Liberal professors are especially enamored of this tactic because it can be used on Christian and conservative students without stepping over the line into blatant persecution or abuse. The point of the tactic is to embarrass those who hold different views so they will be reluctant to express them in the future. Assume your class is discussing the issue of whether America should reinstate the draft (required mandatory military service). A military veteran in your class says, "I joined the Army right after graduating from high school and it was an outstanding experience for me. I think people who oppose the draft might change their minds if they gave military service a chance." Your professor responds with a derisive laugh and says, "Come now, surely you can see how infantile your opinion is. I don't have to murder someone to know that I don't want to do it." As a critical thinker, you might point out that: 1) ridiculing an idea is not the same as refuting it, 2)killing someone is not necessarily murdering him, and 3) in a scholarly environment an idea remains on the table and valid until it can be refuted.

Recognizing the tactics of the radical left explained in this section will help when you are subjected to them. When you stand your ground against a liberal professor, other students, or anyone else using these tactics, remember who you are. Fight back, but do so in a spirit of Christian love. Methods for fighting back, without stooping to the tactics of the left, are explained in the next section.

FIGHT BACK IN A SPIRIT OF CHRISTIAN LOVE

As you read in the previous section, secular humanists will go to great lengths and use disturbing tactics in their attempts to silence Christian and conservative voices on university campuses. In fact, the radical left has shown a willingness to be surprisingly mean-spirited in attacking the worldviews of Christians and conservatives. When this happens to you, the desire to blast your attacker with both barrels— figuratively speaking—is an understandable human reaction. And like many human reactions, this is one you will need to suppress through prayer and self-discipline.

As a Christian, you have a higher level of responsibility in these situations than your secular counterparts. In attempting to advance their views, any tactic that works is acceptable to the radical left. This is not the case with Christians. We too must profess our views and defend them with vigor, but we have to do these things in a spirit of Christian love. God expects us to speak His truth, but in doing so He expects us to reflect the righteousness of His Son. Consequently, you will need to become skilled in the art and science of disagreeing with others without being disagreeable. The following methods will help:

- *Be prepared.* Know your Bible and what it says about the issues of the day—those that are likely to come up in classroom and campus discussions. The radical left has become adept at using the biblical ignorance of Christians against them by distorting what the Bible says, taking verses out of context and misapplying them, and asking believers questions from Scripture they cannot answer. The Bible is a tool God has given us so that we can know Him and help others know Him. Do not allow the radical left to use it as a weapon against God's people. Use what you have been taught in church, Christian school, or homeschool. Stay up-to-date on the issues of the day. Visit the American Vision bookstore (www.americanvision.org) to find the types of books that will help you be prepared.

- *Listen more, talk less.* You learn more from listening than from talking. The beliefs of secular humanists are self-defeating by their very nature. Stripped down to their essentials, these beliefs are built on one simple premise: man is God. Consequently, the beliefs of the left depend on circular reasoning for their validity. If you listen carefully, you will find that secular humanists almost always end up arguing against themselves, especially when they base their assumptions on the concept of moral relativism. You may have heard the maxim about *giving a fool enough rope to hang himself.* This is what you do when you listen to a member of the radical left profess his secular-humanist opinions. Listen long enough and the humanist will eventually give you opportunities for rebuttal big enough to drive a truck through. This is an effective method for dealing with secular humanists, but it is made even more effective by this simple fact: Everyone likes a good listener. This is especially true of liberal academicians who chose higher education as a profession, because it gives them a podium and a built-in audience. If you come to be known as a good listener, you will have far more of opportunities to share your views with liberals who can benefit from them.

- *Use discretion.* You have only so many arrows in your quiver. When going into battle, choose your targets with care and for greatest effect. You do not have to take on every liberal who says something you disagree with. Do this in today's campus environment and you will spend every waking hour debating with liberals. Sometimes you have to just ignore them. It is better to carefully select high-impact opportunities in which advocating or defending your views will have the greatest effect.

- *Be patient.* Your fights against liberal tyranny on campus, as important as they are to you, are really just small skirmishes in a much larger battle. Further, these larger battles on your campus are only a part of an even larger socio-cultural war the left is waging on God, country, and conservatives. Do not feel like you have to win the war all by yourself; be patient. Sometimes the best way to deal with liberals is to ignore them. Further, when you do engage left-leaning professors and students, be patient enough to listen to them. Sometimes the best way to handle a liberal is to simply pray for him. When you do this, do not expect immediate results.

- *Pray before engaging.* When you decide to engage a liberal in a discussion or debate, slow down. Before jumping in with both feet, take the time to say a silent prayer. Ask God for strength, guidance, and the proper motivation. Ask Him to help you reflect the image of His Son as you discuss the issue in question. Winning another convert to Christ is even more important than winning an argument.

- *Control your temper.* As a Christian, if you lose your temper when debating a liberal, you lose period. Often it will be the manner of your speech that brings a liberal around rather than your words. If you feel your temper rising, take a deep breath, say a quick prayer, and do not respond until you have regained control of your emotions. This tactic is the key to being able to disagree without being disagreeable.

- *Commit to disagreeing without being disagreeable.* If you find yourself thinking, "I am going to show this liberal so and so just what's what," stop and examine your motivation. In any conflict with liberal professors and students, your first motivation should be to reflect the righteousness of Christ. Defend your position with vigor, but do so with grace and concern for your adversary. Attack his opinions, but do not attack him. The radical left is determined to stifle Christians and conservatives as part of its campaign for intellectual and ideological conformity. When subjected to persecution by the radical left, you are likely to become angry. When this happens, take a deep breath, say a prayer, and remember that anger will not help you with either of your goals when debating liberals: 1) reflecting Christ in an attempt to show your adversary a better way, and 2) persuading your adversary of the validity of your point of view.

STAND UP TO TEMPTATION

J. Budziszewski tells about being approached by a Christian student who was distraught over the moral challenges of college. "One day a student approached me after class. She seemed to be close to tears. 'In a lecture today, you mentioned that you're a Christian,' she said. 'I've never heard that from any other professor, and every day I spend at this university, I feel my faith is under attack.'"[5] There are going to be times when you will feel the same way, and the reason is simple: your faith is under attack. Nowhere are the attacks more prevalent than on the campuses of colleges and universities.

Much of what you are going to be subjected to in a university environment will run counter to your Christian worldview. There will be opportunities to engage in drinking, drug use, recreational sex, cheating, and other sinful behavior. You will be tempted by a variety of factors—peer pressure, curiosity, the desire to taste forbidden fruit—to participate in activities that are at odds with your beliefs. In these cases, your worst enemy is your own sinful nature. Remember, temptation is Satan's way of appealing to your sinful nature in an attempt to lure you into doing things you should not do.

The first step in standing up to temptation is admitting that you are vulnerable to it. One of the ways Christian college students get into trouble is by thinking that they are immune to the temptations of the world. I have had Christian college students tell me that their faith is strong enough that they can watch R and X-rated movies and not be tempted by the sex and violence, or hang out with friends who use drugs and not be affected. These students thought they could walk through a pigsty without getting mud on their shoes. They were wrong. Maybe some Christians can do these things and not be changed, but most cannot. Christians are just like anyone else, in that we have a sinful nature and Satan knows how to tempt it.

Standing up to the temptations that are ever-present on university campuses will require a concerted effort on your part. What follows are some strategies that will help:

- *Observe others and learn from their mistakes.* A smart man learns from his mistakes, but a wise man learns from the mistakes of others. As you stand up to campus temptations, be wise and learn from the mistakes of others. When you see a fellow Christian student give in to temptation, ask yourself: "In the same situation, what could I have done to avoid his mistake?" Correspondingly, when you see a fellow Christian student successfully turn away from temptation, make note of how he did it, learn from the experience, and congratulate him.

- *Minimize the temptations you are subjected to.* Avoid activities and events that will be temptation intensive. Agreeing to hang out in a bar, attend parties where you know drugs will be used, or spend time alone in a dorm room or apartment with a friend of the opposite sex are decisions that increase temptation. A wiser approach is to minimize your exposure to temptation by refusing to participate in these types of temptation-intensive activities.

- *Use the Bible as your armor against temptation.* When you find yourself being pulled in the wrong direction by temptation, put on the brakes long enough to open your Bible. Find a quiet place and start reading. Focus on verses that deal with temptation. Begin with Matthew 4:1-11 where Christ turns away from the temptations of Satan. Continue this exercise until the urge to give into the temptation passes.

- *Fortify your heart with prayer.* Few things will stop Satan in his tracks so effectively as the prayers of a believer. If you feel pulled in the wrong direction by temptation, fortify your heart with prayer and Satan will flee from you. This is what is meant in James 4:7: "Therefore submit to God. Resist the devil and he will flee from you." A good place to begin is with the Lord's Prayer. Remember that this prayer says: "and lead us not into temptation but deliver us from evil."

- *Do not try to fight temptation alone.* As a Christian you are never alone. Remember this when you must stand up to temptation. God is there and He will help if you go to Him in prayer. In addition, you can find support in an account-ability partner. This is another Christian you can go to, call, or email when you feel temptation getting the upper hand. Your accountability partner is someone you can count on to help you do the right thing when all else has failed. Being a member of a Christian student organization will give you opportunities to find an accountability partner and to be one for another Christian student.

PERSEVERE AGAINST LIBERAL TYRANNY IN ALL OF ITS FORMS

I have talked with Christian and conservative students who retreated into a shell and hid their worldviews away to avoid the abuse of left-leaning college professors. I have also talked with some who simply dropped out of college. Every time a Christian and conservative college student chooses to retreat in these and other ways, the radical left wins a victory. Standing up to the adversity you face in college will not be easy, but doing so will strengthen you for the even bigger culture war that awaits you after college. Liberal tyranny on campus is the focus of this book, but liberal tyranny is not restricted to college and university campuses. It permeates American society. Consequently, one of the most important lessons you can learn in college is how to persevere against liberal tyranny.

Colonel George "Bud" Day

Whenever I discuss the issue of persevering against liberal tyranny with college students, I begin with the true story of Colonel George "Bud" Day, an American hero and Christian, whose life is the best example of persevering against adversity I have ever known. Colonel Day was an Air Force pilot and prisoner of war (POW) during the Vietnam War who received the Medal of Honor for his courageous actions in the face of incredible adversity. Reading Bud Day's story will put the challenges you face in college in their proper perspective, and—I hope—give you the determination to persevere in fighting back against liberal tyranny.

In 1967, Day was a Major in charge of a squadron of F-100 jets nicknamed the Misty Squadron. Day and his pilots served as forward air controllers (FACS) who flew missions over Communist territory in North Vietnam spotting targets for American bombers. On one of these missions, Day's jet was hit by ground fire from the enemy, sending it into a steep dive. Day had just enough time to bail out before the jet crashed into the dense jungle of North Vietnam. In the process of ejecting, Day was thrown against the fuselage of the jet, breaking his arm. His parachute opened in time, but it brought him down into the waiting arms of the enemy. Upon landing, Day twisted his knee making it difficult for him to walk.

Fully aware of Day's painful injuries, the enemy guerillas forced him to walk for miles through the jungle to their camp. Upon arriving at the camp, Day's captors began to interrogate him. They wanted to know when the next American airstrike would come, from what direction, and how many aircraft would be involved. When Day refused to tell them anything, the torture began. The enemy's methods were brutal. They included hanging an already badly injured Day upside down and beating him. When even this failed to break the courageous pilot, the enemy guerillas staged an execution that, as far as Day knew, was going to be the real thing.

The guerillas forced Day into a kneeling position and placed a pistol against his head. Day heard the ominous click as the pistol was cocked. Convinced he was about to die, Day thought one last time of his wife, Doris, and said a silent prayer. Just before pulling the trigger, the executioner turned the pistol away just enough to ensure that the bullet he fired missed. It did, but just barely. In fact, the pistol was fired so close to Day's ear that he experienced temporary deafness and a permanently damaged eardrum.

In spite of this cruel hoax, his painful injuries, and the brutal torture, Bud Day persevered in resisting. He steadfastly refused to give in to his captors. The torture continued for several days until it appeared that the battered and bloodied pilot could not possibly live, much less escape. It was at this point that the guards made the mistake of presuming too much. By now they should have known the type of man they were dealing with, but they did not yet get it. One night the guards failed to watch their stubborn prisoner as closely as they should have, and he slipped quietly into the jungle and escaped. It was hours before the enemy realized that their prize had escaped. In the meantime, Day had used those hours to put as much distance as possible between himself and his captors.

Once he had gained a sufficient head start, the battered pilot began sleeping in jungle thickets during the daylight hours and running during the safer night hours. After about 48 hours on the run, Day was sleeping in a jungle thicket, trying to preserve his failing strength, when he was startled awake by an ear-splitting explosion. An American jet had dropped a bomb or fired a missile—no doubt intended for Day's pursuers—that exploded nearby, driving jagged shards of hot shrapnel deep into his leg.

Day's ever-growing catalog of injuries now included a broken arm, sprained knee, and assorted wounds from the shrapnel and torture; wounds that without treatment were rapidly becoming infected in the filthy jungle environment. In spite of these mounting injuries, Day continued to slowly and painfully hobble in a southerly direction. His goal was to reach friendly territory in South Vietnam and rejoin his squadron. But his festering wounds, debilitating injuries, harsh jungle environment, and a lack of food and water were beginning to take their toll.

After ten or more days on the run (Day lost track) with little food or water, he was also suffering from dehydration and hunger. In spite of the pain, loss of blood, hunger, and thirst, he persevered. With every ounce of strength he could muster, the determined pilot continued his trek south toward freedom. Then, one day he heard the sound of helicopters. Knowing they had to be American, Day hobbled toward the noise, a noise that to him meant freedom. All that now separated Day from a U.S. Marine Corps fire-support base and the freedom it represented was a river—or at least that is what he thought at the time.

Upon closer examination, Day could see that the jungle along the river's edge was teeming with Vietcong guerillas. He was now only a mile or so from freedom, but these last steps on his tortuous journey would turn out to be the most heartbreakingly difficult of them all. With all of the patience and stealth he could muster, Day crawled down to the river's edge and slipped quietly into the water. Taking advantage of a log floating by, he used it for cover to float undetected down the river. When he had floated far enough down river that he could no longer see any enemy guerillas, Day crawled ashore on what he believed was the freedom side of the river. He was starving, dehydrated, weak from the loss of blood, and exhausted almost beyond endurance, but full of hope. With the little remaining strength he could muster, Day began making his way toward the American fire-support base.

He never made it. As Day hobbled toward freedom, hope growing with every step, he stumbled right into a Vietcong ambush. Shots were fired and Day was hit in the hand and the leg by rounds from an AK-47. He lay on the jungle floor unable to move. After persevering so courageously for two weeks in the worst possible conditions, Day was recaptured in sight of the American base that would have meant freedom. His flight from captivity was over, and an even worse ordeal was about to begin.

Day's captors returned him to the same camp from which he had escaped two weeks earlier. But this time the guerillas had a better idea of the type of person they were dealing with. Rather than waste time trying to torture him into submission, the guerillas shipped Day off to the Hanoi Hilton, the infamous POW camp in the capital of North Vietnam. It would be years before Bud Day would once again breathe the fresh air of freedom.

When Day arrived at the Hanoi Hilton, he was suffering from malnutrition, dehydration, infected wounds, exhaustion, and blood loss. In response to the pain he had endured from torture and his assorted untreated injuries, Day's hands had curled tightly into claws that he could not open. When he was tossed unceremoniously onto the hard, damp, concrete floor of his prison cell, Day could neither feed nor dress himself. Thus began a period of systematic torture, privation, and abuse that would last five years—a period in which Day's character, courage, and determination would be tested daily in ways most people cannot even imagine.

Having thrown Day into a cell, his captors simply left him. They thought, no doubt, they were leaving him to die. Once again they had underestimated the courage, perseverance, and commitment of this American patriot. With the help of his cell mates, Day was eventually able to regain the use of his hands sufficiently to dress and feed himself. In addition, his broken bones and wounds slowly began to heal, although he would suffer lifelong bouts of pain from the harsh treatment he endured as a POW.

As one of the senior officers in his cell block, Day knew it was incumbent on him to set an example of resistance for the other POWs. Day vowed to himself and God that he would never give in to his communist tormentors, never quit setting an example for his men, and endure whatever he had to in order to maintain his honor as an Air Force officer and his dignity as a human being. He would pay a heavy price for this courageous stand, but he stuck steadfastly to his vow, even in situations that just went from bad to worse, and there were plenty of those.

Day's determination to persevere extended beyond just his personal resistance. He also worked hard to help his fellow POWs resist their brutal captors. To give his men the hope they needed to endure an ordeal that seemed to have no end, Day and a few other officers began conducting worship services, an act strictly forbidden in a POW camp where atheism was the official policy. Day and his fellow Christians knew they were taking a chance that could have deadly results. But their love of God and country and their need for hope were stronger than their fear of torture and death. The worship services became a regular, albeit covert, part of their routine.

One day in the middle of a worship service, North Vietnamese guards suddenly burst into the cell with rifles loaded, aimed, and ready to fire. This was the moment of truth. Day knew the guards would have no qualms about shooting American POWs, but he also knew that leadership demanded a strong stand on his part. Not hesitating for a moment, Day stood up, faced the guards who were now pointing their weapons at him, and began singing America's national anthem. Moved by Day's courageous example, the other POWs joined in and made it a chorus. The communist guards were so stunned by this simple act of courage and independence that they did not know how to react. The air in the cell was electric with tension. It was a situation in which anything could happen. After what seemed like an eternity, but was in fact just seconds, the guards finally lowered their weapons and backed out of the cell. Rather than shoot the prisoners, they opted for their favorite solution to any problem with the POWs—

torture. Grasping Day and another officer, the guards led them away to a fate every POW knew about.

Day and his fellow POWs were finally released from captivity on March 14, 1973. Thus ended a five-year ordeal for Day that few people will ever experience and even fewer could endure. Through it all—the torture, abuse, and mental cruelty—Day had courageously persevered. He never gave up and never gave in. As a result of his ordeal, Day received the Medal of Honor—our nation's highest award for valor in combat.

Colonel Day had faith in Christ, faith that God is in control of history, and belief in the rightness of the cause for which he fought. He also knew that he had the fellowship of other like-minded people who were suffering through the same ordeal. Christian and conservative students have the same assurances. Christian and conservative college students are likely to experience adversity on university campuses as a result of liberal tyranny. It might amount to nothing more than minor harassment or it could come in the form of persecution, intimidation, and other even more serious types of abuse. It might take the form of rejection by secular humanists, pressure from left-leaning professors, or even threats from anonymous sources. When you must face adversity during your college years—regardless of what form it takes—recall this story about Colonel Bud Day and all he endured. His example of courage and perseverance will help you endure your trials.

Stand Up To Adversity

As a Christian or conservative in an institution dominated by the left, you should take it as a given that you will experience adversity. This fact should be understood before deciding to pursue a college education. Learning how to stand up to adversity will be critical to your success in college. Those who lose faith when they encounter roadblocks, detours, and potholes on the road to success will never succeed.

According to Pastor Voddie Baucham, Jr.,

> The Christian life that is void of suffering has never experienced real growth. It has never seen the end of itself and the remarkable grace of the intervening hand of

God. It has never done the undoable, seen the unimaginable, or received the unattainable. The Christian life that has not seen suffering does not truly know that God is able, that He is good, that He is always right on time, that He is larger than our greatest fears, that He is nearer than the wind on our faces.[6]

Since adversity is likely to be part of your college experience, it follows that you should know how to stand up to it. The following strategies will help:

- *Remember that God has a purpose for your suffering.* God uses adversity to strengthen His saints, as is shown in Romans 5:3-5: "We also exult in our tribulations knowing that tribulation brings perseverance; and perseverance, proven character; and proven character, hope; and hope does not disappoint." Learning to stand up to the adversity you experience in college is part of God's plan to strengthen you for even bigger challenges in the future.

- *Use adversity to bring you closer to God.* Never make the mistake of letting adversity drive a wedge between you and God. I have had frustrated Christian students tell me that college would be a breeze if it weren't for their beliefs. This is why some hide their beliefs during college. This is a mistake. Let the challenges of pursuing a college education in a left-leaning university drive you closer to God. As humans we are frail, but with God we can gain the strength to persevere just as Colonel Bud Day did for almost five years as a POW.

- *Remember that you are not alone in your adversity.* When you have just been forced to endure a distasteful encounter with an overbearing leftist professor, it is easy to think that you are alone. You are not. There may be other like-minded students in your class who are afraid to speak out. There are certainly others on campus. 2 Timothy 3:12 says: "All who desire to live Godly in Christ Jesus will be persecuted." Seek out fellow Christians on campus who have suffered because of their faith but persevered, learn from their experience, and grow from their wisdom. This is one of the reasons we recommend that you join a Christian student organization while in college. These organizations will bring you together on a regular basis with Christians who are facing or have faced the same challenges you are facing. Just knowing that you are not alone will bolster your spirit and your resolve.

- *Refuse to give in to adversity.* Use the Bible, prayer, and the suffering of others to keep the adversity you face in college in proper perspective. Doing this will give you the strength to keep going when you feel like giving up. God is bigger than the problems you will face in college. He knows what you are facing and how much you can take. God is like the coach who knows that athletes must suffer through the pain of being pushed to their physical, mental, and emotional limits if they are going to excel. Rely on God to be your coach during times of adversity—He knows your limits.

- *Reach out to someone else who is being persecuted.* One of the best ways to help yourself during times of adversity is to help someone else. Invariably, when we reach out to others who are bearing burdens we gain a more positive and thankful perspective. No matter how much we are suffering, we find that there are others who are hurting even more. In times of adversity during your college years, help yourself through it by helping others.

- *Take the long view.* In times of adversity it is easy to get caught up in the pain of the moment and think that our problems will never end. They will. Consequently, it will help if you take the long view. When you feel like the pressure to conform to a liberal worldview will never end, remember what it says in Romans 8:28: "And we know that all things work together for the good of those who love God, to those who are called according to His purpose." Cling to God in times of trouble and you will eventually emerge from it stronger and better.

GO ON THE OFFENSIVE
AGAINST LIBERAL TYRANNY

In the book *The Conservative Guide to Campus Activism*, Jason Mattera asserts that,

> You can either be a mediocre and average college student, or you can approach every semester with a sense of purpose and destiny, dedicating your energy and time to confronting liberalism and spreading conservatism.[7]

This is an excellent point. Christians in secular settings spend a lot of time defending their faith, and conservatives in settings dominated by liberals spend a lot of time defending their beliefs. In the Marine Corps, we were taught the following maxim: *The best defense is a strong offense.* We learned that you should never just sit back and take what the enemy throws at you. Instead, turn the tables on your adversary by going on the offensive. What follows are some strategies for going on the offensive:

- Engage the left in debates

- Start a conservative student organization

- Host Christian and conservative speakers and events

Engaging the Left in Debates

The radical left functions best when it can broadcast one-way tirades against God, country, and conservatives. Inflicting uncontested diatribes on a captive audience is easy. Anyone can win a one-sided fight. Things are different when left-leaning professors and students are challenged and must defend their views. This is one of the reasons the radical left wants to silence Christian and conservative college students. Engaging the left in debates is an effective way to go on the offensive, but in order for this strategy to bear fruit you must be well-prepared. Never go into battle unarmed. Bay Buchanan recommends the following tactics for engaging the left in debate:

- *Define your goal.* Do not undertake a debate without first deciding what you want to accomplish. Do you want to convert your opponent, impress the audience, balance the discussion, antagonize the opposition, or just make sure that the Christian and conservative point of view is heard? Do you want to reveal the shortcomings of secular humanism and moral relativism? Your goal determines the approach you will take in the debate.

- *Use non-verbal communication to best advantage.* A substantial part of communication is non-verbal. One of the reasons Vice-President Nixon did better on the radio than on television when debating John F. Kennedy during the presidential election of 1960, was that listeners could not see him. Those who watched the debate on television observed Nixon sending all of the wrong non-verbal messages. He did not smile and so appeared mean-spirited. He kept furtively glancing at Kennedy, instead of maintaining eye contact with the audience. He fidgeted and appeared nervous. Declining professional help with his make-up, Nixon appeared haggard and in need of a shave. All of these non-verbal mistakes hurt him. But on the radio, listeners gave Nixon the edge over Kennedy because they were not distracted by negative non-verbal messages. When you debate someone, remember these non-verbal tactics: 1) look at the audience, 2) maintain a friendly demeanor, or at least one that is non-aggressive, 3) speak with conviction about your beliefs (passive, disinterested monotones are not persuasive, but on the other hand neither are loud, boisterous, or mean-spirited comments), 4) stand up straight and make a conscious effort to avoid nervous affectations (uh, um, jiggling change in your pockets, white-knuckling the podium), 5) use self-effacing humor when possible, but avoid humor that puts down or embarrasses your opponent, and 6) dress up for the occasion (this will show respect for the audience, the issues, and your opponent).

- *Prepare, prepare, prepare.* Never go into battle unarmed. Study the issues to be debated from your point of view and from your opponent's. Ideally you should know your opponent's views and facts better than he does. Further, you should know your side of the issue so well that your opponent cannot use the same tactic on you. Again, this is where American Vision can help (www.americanvision.org).

- *Avoid drowning the audience in facts and figures.* Having a few carefully-selected facts and figures ready to use at an appropriate moment is good debating strategy. However, drowning the audience and your opponent in a tidal wave of facts will just win him points with listeners. Use enough facts to show that you know your topic, but not so many that you sound like an accountant talking to the IRS. Audiences respond better to illustrative stories than to long recitations of data.

- *Make an outline of key points and reminders.* An outline will help you stay focused and on message. Do not try to memorize what you plan to say. There are several reasons for this: 1) you will get nervous and forget, 2) you will sound stiff and scripted, and 3) your opponent might catch you off guard by introducing information not covered in your script. It is better to appear natural, well-informed, and comfortable with your material.

- *Speak from the heart.* If you do not appear to believe in your views, why should the audience? Do not overdo it, but show the audience—verbally and non-verbally—that you are interested in what you are saying and believe it to be the truth.

- *Practice before engaging.* A bright general once said that even the best plan will not survive contact with the enemy. Another way to express the same principle is that things seldom turn out exactly the way you think they will. Flexibility is an important asset for debaters. It allows you to be quick on your feet, or at least appear to be. Some people are naturally this way, but most are not. This is why it is important to practice often before actually engaging in debate. By practice, we mean discussing the issues to be debated with fellow Christians and conservatives and asking them to play the role of the opposition. In presidential debates, both candidates practice by having staff members and other experts pose the questions they think the opposition might raise during the debate. You do not want to let yourself be caught flat-footed during a debate and have to admit, "I never thought of that."[8]

Start a Conservative Student Organization

Most universities have Christian student organizations, but this is not the case with conservative student organizations. If your university does not have a student organization dedicated to advancing a conservative worldview, start one. We recommend affiliating with an established national organization. This approach can provide several advantages, including access to services, training, speakers, publications, publicity, by-laws, and conferences. It also provides a national support base that can be invaluable in assisting with both start-up challenges and on-going operations.

Host Christian and Conservative Speakers and Events

Universities frequently host special events with prominent speakers from different fields. Exposing students to the diverse views of leading thinkers from different fields is part of what a university should do. Further, participating in these types of events is supposed to be part of the college experience for students. However, in universities dominated by the radical left, special events with speakers are typically designed to advance the liberal agenda. The majority of these events support the causes of the radical left (*i.e.* gun control, abortion, gay rights, etc.). One of the best ways to fight back against liberal tyranny is to organize campus events with Christian and conservative speakers.

If your university does not provide balance in the special events it offers, do it yourself. Not only is this a good way to fight back, it will enhance your education and that of your fellow students. Commenting on why it is important for students to invite conservative speakers to their university, David Horowitz said:

> You can't get a good education if they're only telling you half the story. But it is especially important for conservative students who will benefit tremendously from the reinforcement and example provided by conservative speakers.[9]

If you are a member of a Christian or conservative student organization, it can be helpful in organizing events and arranging speakers. This is one of the reasons we recommend joining student organizations that have a national affiliation. The key is to begin by identifying your institution's procedures for organizing events and inviting speakers. Know the bureaucracy and how it works. If you are a Christian and conservative student, dealing with your university should be approached like dealing with the IRS—know their rules better than they do. The university may try to passively kill your proposed event by burying it in red tape and paperwork.

The university's guidelines for organizing special events are published in either its catalog or its student handbook. Follow established procedures to the letter. Do not let haphazard planning on your part give the university a legitimate reason to deny approval of the proposed event. Be persistent and do not back down or give up. If you find yourself dealing with a university official who is obviously trying to block the event, in spite of your having followed established procedures, contact the national chapter of your student organization or the Alliance Defense Fund (www.alliancedefensefund.org).

As a college student, you are on the front line in the fight against liberal tyranny on campus. If this sounds daunting, just keep in mind the material explained in this chapter. You can survive your college experience with your Christian and conservative worldview unscathed, provided you know what to expect and respond appropriately. Responding appropriately means being a critical thinker, standing up to temptation, persevering, fighting back in a spirit of Christian love, committing to being a part of campus life without compromising your principles, and going on the offensive. Do these things and you will not just survive the fight with the radical left, you will win it. Having said this, do not get so absorbed in fighting back that you neglect your studies. Never give the left ammunition in the form of bad grades and incomplete classes. You will have more credibility with your fellow Christians, conservatives, undecided students, and the left, if you excel as a student.

NOTES

1. Project Pushback, "Pro-Marriage speech garners professor's wrath." Retrieved from http://onenewsnow.com/Legal/Default.aspx?id=422144 on February 16, 2009.

2. Daniel Feldman, *Critical Thinking* (Menlo Park, CA: Drisp Learning, 2002).

3. Feldman, *Critical Thinking*.

4. Feldman, *Critical Thinking*.

5. J. Budziszewski, *How to Stay Christian in College* (Colorado Springs: NavPress, 2004), 17.

6. Voddie Baucham, Jr., *The Everloving Truth* (Nashville, TN: Lifeway Press, 2006), 88.

7. Jason Mattera, "The Activist Mentality," in Patrick X. Cayle and Ron Robinson, *The Conservative Guide to Campus Activism* (Herndon, VA: Young America's Foundation, 2005), 1.

8. Bay Buchanan, "The Art of Debate," in Patrick X. Cayle and Ron Robinson, *The Conservative Guide to Campus Activism* (Herndon, VA: Young America's Foundation, 2005), 10-13.

9. David Horowitz as quoted in Patrick X. Cayle and Ron Robinson, *The Conservative Guide to Campus Activism* (Herndon, VA: Young America's Foundation, 2005), 83.

Eight

A Final Word on Liberal Tyranny

"When men are pure, laws are useless;
when men are corrupt, laws are broken."
—Benjamin Disraeli

I f you step back and view American culture from a broad perspective, the socio-cultural decline in our country since the end of World War II is startling and disturbing. In every aspect of American life, the radical left has made unquestionable inroads—inroads that have taken our country farther and farther down a one-way street to destruction. Rick Scarborough sums up the current situation in America in his book, *Enough is Enough:*

> America needs a healing. The evidence of that need is everywhere you turn now: failing schools, rampant immorality, broken homes, violent crime, exploitation of children, pornography, a faltering economy, loss of jobs—all leading to growing despair and hopelessness. Empowered by their many successes over the past seventy years and the inability of the Right to stop them, the Left is now ready to move in for the final solution: the criminalization of Christianity and the silencing of the confessing church.[1]

One of the principal battlegrounds in the radical left's war against God, country, and conservatives is the university campus. It is here that left-leaning faculties, aided and abetted by university administrators, make their most concerted efforts to dominate American society. Their strategies include: 1) giving the most radical elements of the left an open microphone while drowning out the voices of Christians and conservatives, 2) using pressure, intimidation, persecution, and abuse to promote intellectual conformity, while discouraging scholarly inquiry that runs counter to liberal orthodoxy, 3) using secular humanism disguised as scholarship to turn Christian and conservative students away from their core beliefs, 4) turning naïve young people who have never learned to think critically into budding liberals, and 5) using their position of dominance to silence Christian and conservative dissent.

The radical left has become increasingly strident and open in its denunciations of traditional American values, especially those based in Christianity. For example, noted atheist Sam Harris—a favorite of the radical left—comments on what he calls the "lunatic influence of religious belief."[2] His message is clear: Christians are misguided lunatics to be pitied rather than taken seriously in the marketplace of ideas.

The left has also become more aggressive in its efforts to strip naïve young Christians of their core beliefs. Dinesh D'Souza comments on the use of sex by atheists to lure college students away from the flock:

> A second strategy commonly used to promote atheism on campus utilizes the vehicle of adolescent sexuality. Atheism is promoted as a means for young people to liberate themselves from moral constraint and indulge their appetites. Religion, in this framework, is portrayed as a form of sexual repression.[3]

AMERICAN CULTURE: THEN AND NOW

Socio-cultural changes occur so gradually that many fail to realize they are even happening. This is the phenomenon known as *boiling-the-frog,* a favorite strategy of the left. It is only by making then-versus-now comparisons that we can come to appreciate just how much American culture has changed over the years. For example, when I was a child divorce was practically unheard of. When my parents divorced in 1959, almost overnight I became an oddity among my friends. In fact, some parents would no longer allow their children to play with me. It was as if I had contracted a contagious disease. Now if children were not allowed to play with friends who have divorced parents, they would have few playmates at all.

Public schools used to operate hand-in-hand with parents and families. The values taught at home were reinforced at school. Teachers did not think they had the right to overrule or undermine parents. Students were responsible for their schoolwork and behavior and were held accountable for both. In disagreements between school officials and students, parents invariably sided with the school. My sixth-grade teacher was thin and elderly, but my classmates and I would not have dared to defy her authority. She had the backing of the school, our parents, and the community. She knew this, and we did too.

I attended public elementary schools for grades one through six and every school day began with a Bible reading, the Lord's Prayer, and the Pledge of Allegiance. Christianity was the norm. I can remember being called on the carpet by public school teachers for skipping Sunday school or church. There was no need denying my truancy either because they knew—they were there. In high school I played football. Before taking the field, we knelt in the locker room and listened in reverent silence as our coach prayed for us. Then, before the opening kickoff, a local minister would pray over the stadium's public address system. All of the spectators in the stands stood and bowed their heads. Today you would have to look long and hard to find a public school willing to defy the ACLU and allow, much less require, Bible reading and prayer before class.

Neighborhoods were much different when I was growing up. We did not lock our doors, other parents in the neighborhood felt comfortable correcting our bad behavior, and we could play outside unsupervised all day without fear of pedophiles, drug pushers, or child abusers. In fact, during the summer months, our parents expected us to "go outside and play" after breakfast and not return until lunch.

The routine was repeated after lunch. We could range far and wide in our neighborhood with no thought of danger, all the while knowing that if we stepped out of line an adult would be on the telephone to our parents within minutes.

Today, adults are actually afraid to confront miscreant youth; if not attacked by the youth themselves, they will probably be sued by their helicopter parents. Not only do families lock their doors these days, many have installed expensive security systems, and with good reason. Home intrusions and break-ins have become common crimes in most communities, especially upper-middle class and wealthy neighborhoods where predatory youth use burglary to finance their drug habits. Telling your children to "go out and play and be back by supper" is unheard of these days.

Rick Scarborough asks a pertinent question about the past versus the present state of affairs in America: "How could we go from a society where divorce was almost nonexistent, the church was the center of the community, the school's greatest discipline problems were talking and chewing gum, and neighborhoods seldom witnessed 'for sale' signs to a society where divorce has become the rule, church is considered irrelevant, schools are installing metal detectors, and the average family moves twelve times in only forty years?" The answer to Scarborough's question is found in the creeping secularization of American society. As a country, we have turned from the religion of God to the religion of secular humanism. We have given up biblical values and embraced moral relativism.

A FINAL WORD ON LIBERAL TYRANNY

The radical left has won a series of victories in the culture war which it is waging against God, country, and conservatives. The American family has been shattered, our public schools have been turned into leftist indoctrination centers, and the church is reeling from the effects of liberal theology, not to mention the sordid state of affairs in the entertainment industry—one of the left's most effective weapons. With these victories in place, the radical left is now focused on one of its most cherished prizes: higher education.

The left knows that if it can control the faculties, administrations, and curriculums of our nation's institutions of higher education, it can control the minds of America's next generation of leaders. Christians and conservatives cannot allow this to happen. Every victory of the left mentioned in this book has been aided by Christians and conservatives who chose to retreat rather than stand and fight. We cannot afford to retreat any longer. It is time to fight back. Making Americans aware of the critical need to take a stand and equipping them to fight back is the purpose of this book.

This book is not just for college students and their parents. It is for all Americans who are concerned about the leftist tidal wave that has swept across our country, covering society in the detritus of moral decay. If you are concerned about America's future and want to take a stand, the college or university campus is a good place to start. It is here that your efforts have the most potential to bear fruit. The left understands this and is acting accordingly. Consequently, it is critical that Christians and conservatives take up the cause and fight back.

NOTES

1. Rick Scarborough, *Enough Is Enough* (Lake Mary, FL: Front Line, 2004), 6.

2. Sam Harris, *The End of Faith: Religion, Terror, and the Future of Reason* (New York: W.W. Norton, 2005), 234.

3. Dinesh D'Souza, *What's So Great About Christianity* (Washington, DC: Regnery Publishing, 2007), 36.

4. Scarborough, *Enough is Enough*, 31.

Printed in the United States
219726BV00002B/1/P

9 780984 064120